Michael Furnell

THE
STAMP
COLLECTORS
ALMANAC

Bloomsbury Books · London

First published by Lochar Publishing Ltd.
Moffat, Scotland DG10 9ED.

This edition published by Bloomsbury Books, an imprint of
The Godfrey Cave Group, 42 Bloomsbury Street, London, WC1B 3QJ,
under licence from Eric Dobby Publishing Ltd,
12 Warnford Road, Orpington, Kent BR6 6LW, 1993

Postage stamps illustrated in this publication by kind
permission of Royal Mail Stamps, London EC1M 5NS
and the Jersey and Guernsey Postal authorities.

Printed and bound in Great Britain by
BPCC Hazell Books Ltd

Member of BPCC Ltd

ISBN 1 85471 312 4

CONTENTS

INTRODUCTION

I have been a stamp collector for over 50 years. As a boy I collected mainly British Colonials of the George Vth and VIth eras, including the 'Omnibus' issues for the Silver Jubilee and Coronation. I was helped by my father who gave me stamps from his firm's mail and also provided some extra pocket money to encourage me to concentrate on my hobby.

Without doubt my interest in stamps helped my education, for my most successful subjects in examinations at school were geography and history.

Soon after leaving school I joined the Navy and spent a year shorebased in Italy where I soon became interested in stamps of that country and in Allied Occupation issues.

After the war, a busy career in journalism meant that I had less time for stamps and so I restricted my collecting to the issues of Great Britain commencing with the Penny Black, which I believe is still the most dignified stamp ever issued and only rivalled perhaps by the four definitives issued at the beginning of 1990 which depicted the heads of Queen Victoria and Queen Elizabeth II.

I now have an almost complete collection of the stamps issued by Great Britain since 1840 and from these I have chosen to illustrate and write up briefly about 100 stamps, mostly commemoratives, which in my opinion are of special interest.

This almanac, like others in the series, is intended to appeal to those who would like to find out some essential information about a subject, without ploughing through highly technical reference books. Thus *The Stamp Collectors Almanac* does not delve deeply into phosphor bands or stamps impregnated with phosphorescent substances for the benefit of electronic cancelling machinery, or graphite lines or other technicalities.

Some simple guidance is given in the 'Glossary of Philatelic Terms' at the back of the book, otherwise most pages are devoted to illustrations and a chronicle of interesting stamps issued by this country over the past century and a half.

I have used the term 'scarcity' throughout the listings with some caution, for almost all the stamps issued by Great Britain have achieved sales of a million copies or more and some have passed the one hundred million mark, but of course many of these have not survived, having been used on commercial mail and destroyed on receipt.

The values I have quoted must be approximate as dealers sometimes make special offers and at other times find certain items in short supply and therefore increase their charges, if only temporarily.

I have enjoyed compiling this book and hope that my readers will find it useful and informative.

Michael Furnell
October 1991

THE HOBBY OF STAMP COLLECTING

The very first adhesive postage stamp was issued on 6 May 1840 by Great Britain. This was the famous One Penny Black and it was closely followed two days later by the Two Pence Blue.

These stamps were issued for Rowland Hill's new Uniform Penny Post scheme. This provided for the carriage of letters in the UK by the Post Office, at the rate of one penny per half ounce, irrespective of the distance covered for the delivery. The sender prepaid the cost by affixing one or more of the new stamps to the letter. Previously the charge had depended on the mileage to be covered, the weight of the item and the number of pages it contained. Furthermore the recipient had to pay the charge.

The new service immediately became very popular and the amount of mail carried by the Post Office increased considerably.

The hobby of stamp collecting seems to have commenced very quickly, for in 1841 a letter appeared in a London newspaper asking readers to send used postage stamps to a young lady who was making a collection of them.

At that time there were only four postage stamps in existence, namely the Penny Black, Two Pence Blue of 1840 and their successors, the Penny Red and Two Pence Blue with lines, which were issued early in the following year.

It was not until 1843 that any other country followed Britain's example and in that year Brazil and the Swiss cantons of Geneva and Zurich produced adhesive postage stamps, closely followed by Basle (Switzerland) in 1845, plus Mauritius and the USA two years later.

Thus in the early days most collectors tended to accumulate lots of similar stamps and as there were no special albums available, they often gummed them into exercise books. Some even covered chairs, tables or walls of rooms as adornments, or even made decorative fire-screens with patterns of stamps.

After a while these pioneer collectors began to take more care of their accumulations and when stamps from foreign countries began to become available, they started to realise that some items were issued in very small quantities and therefore more desirable than those that were more common.

The collecting instinct was helped by the appearance of the first stamp album around 1862 and this was followed by Stanley Gibbons first price list and catalogue of stamps which was published in 1865.

Gibbons was a pioneer stamp dealer, whose destiny it might be thought, was to promote stamp collecting as a hobby, for he was born on 21 June 1840, just a few weeks after the arrival of the Penny Black. He became interested in stamps while still at school.

His father ran a chemist's shop in Plymouth and when he had completed his education Stanley joined his parent in the business, but soon realised the potential of his hobby and began dealing in stamps from a corner of the shop.

Stamp trading soon overtook pharmaceuticals and he became a full-time dealer in philately. In 1863 he had a stroke of good fortune when two sailors offered him a large kitbag of triangular stamps from the Cape of Good Hope which they had won in a raffle while in South Africa. He is reputed to have delighted the men when he paid them £5 for the accumulation. This was probably a milestone in his business career, for it is claimed he later reckoned to have made £500 profit from the deal.

He moved to London in 1874 and built up a prosperous business with the aid of his brother Alfred who was a naval officer and helped him with worldwide contacts for the supply of stamps, during his travels.

As a rich man he decided to retire in 1890 and see the world, so he sold his firm to Charles Phillips, a Birmingham businessman for £25,000. Phillips moved the business to London's Strand in 1893. The firm still has a shop and offices in this street and is one of the best known philatelic dealers in the world.

THE FASCINATION OF COLLECTING

There is no doubt that early collectors found the hobby of great interest and a relief from the humdrum existence of life for many in the middle of the nineteenth century.

Today there are many other distractions and hobbies to keep us amused in our leisure hours, but probably no other pastime can offer such a diverse range of opportunities for learning in a very pleasant way.

The study of stamps can improve one's knowledge of history, politics, geography, the arts, transportation, literature, aviation, horticulture, printing, sport and the theatre, to name just a few of the many subjects covered by stamps which have been issued during the past century and a half.

FORMING A COLLECTION

In the early days many collectors tried to obtain all the stamps that had been issued irrespective of the subjects, origins or values. This was not easy and gradually became almost impossible to achieve due to the rarity of some issues and the fact that worldwide communications were far more crude than they are today, so it was often awkward to obtain information on the latest emissions.

Fifty years ago there were still plenty of enthusiasts who formed general collections containing all the more common stamps of the major and many minor countries all over the globe. Then specialisation began, with collectors concentrating their efforts on groups of countries such as the British Colonies, Europe, Africa, Asia, Australasia, the Pacific Islands or North and South America.

In the last decade of the twentieth century it is even more necessary to specialise, for there are over 283,000 stamps, from 1840 to date, listed in the latest Gibbons simplified catalogue *Stamps of the World* and in 1990 alone about ten thousand new stamps were issued throughout the world.

Thus specialisation is essential unless one has an inexhaustible bank balance. Some people only acquire mint or used new issues of a small group of countries, others prefer to buy first day covers (envelopes bearing stamps postmarked on the first day of issue). Collecting the stamps issued in the reign of Queen Victoria, King George V, or our present Queen, from a small number of British Commonwealth countries is another popular group. Dedicated enthusiasts will devote all their efforts into research about one particular stamp, such as the Penny Black, and will delve deeply into the various printings, postmarks and variations available.

Diversity is the keynote to stamp collecting, for there are no strict rules which say you must form a collection in any particular way - you just please yourself.

OTHER SPECIALISATIONS

Thematic collecting is a popular branch of the hobby in these days. Hobbyists who concentrate on this aspect form accumulations of stamps devoted to one particular topic or subject. For instance a very attractive collection can be made devoted to flowers and trees on stamps. Other themes can include railways, sport, ships, aircraft, youth organisations, religion, music and even stamps on stamps. The scope is almost unlimited and there is no need to restrict one's activities to one country or continent. The cost of forming a thematic collection can be relatively modest, for many of the modern stamps are available at not much over face value.

Postal history is a fast growing branch of the hobby and a fascinating one. Some historians will delve into the development of postal services in their own home town or a country of particular interest to them. Others will trace the development of airmails to say the Far East or the activities of Foreign Post Offices in China at the turn of the century. The history of the post in Antarctica is another popular subject and even non-philatelic material may be sought, such as photographs of penguins or a base camp.

Accumulating errors on stamps is an activity which has devotees. In many cases modern errors are in effect printers' waste, which should never have been released to the public if the sophisticated checking procedures had been one hundred percent effective. Nevertheless, some philatelists are prepared to pay considerable sums for a stamp which has not been perforated properly or one with a missing colour or emblem. Mistakes were more justified in the early days of stamp production. For example the aeroplane on the 1918 USA airmail 24 cent stamp was printed upside down, due to the fact that one sheet of stamps was placed into the printing press the wrong way up when the second colour was machined. This was not noticed by the Overseer and it is believed that only one hundred copies were released. Thus the stamp is scarce and is now considered to be quite valuable.

In 1991 a record price was realised at auction by Harmers in Switzerland for a Penny Black on cover, postmarked 2 May 1840, which was four days before the stamps were officially released. A Japanese buyer paid £1.35 million for this item.

Collecting postmarks is another interesting sideline. Much can be learnt about postal services and destinations from the cancellation marks on early stamps of Great Britain (and other countries). Initially the Maltese Cross handstamp was made in bulk for the Post Office, but later some were made by hand individually so they vary slightly and specialists are able to identify the office of origin in many cases. From 1844 numeral obliterators were introduced, which again can be identified as to origin.

Currently a very wide range of postmarks are used in many parts of the world. Some are for special events, while others are used for advertising purposes. These appeal to specialist collectors.

Those interested in typography and graphic arts make a study of the design and printing of stamps and there is much data now available on these subjects from most postal authorities. For earlier issues detailed research is sometimes necessary.

Forgeries appeal to some individuals. These were more common in the past when printing was not so technically advanced. Sometimes these illegal issues were produced to defraud the postal authorities, but quite often the intention has been to deceive stamp collectors by producing imitations of valuable stamps. All forgeries ought to have an indication of their status indelibly marked on the reverse side.

Stamps that are not stamps are sometimes described as 'Cinderellas' and there are collectors who find much satisfaction in accumulating these items. In the main they comprise patriotic labels, greetings stamps, small advertising labels, labels to raise funds for charities, fiscals and exhibition souvenirs. None of these are valid for the prepayment of postage, but they form an interesting and quite cheap sideline.

Among other specialisations which appeal to certain collectors are stamps issued for official or government correspondence, airmail stamps, postage due issues for underpaid or non-paid postage and duty and revenue stamps.

MOUNTING AND ARRANGING A COLLECTION

One of the advantages of collecting stamps is that you can arrange all the items in any way you wish. There is a vast range of stamp albums for sale through stamp dealers, stationers and bookshops. These start at simple books of say 64 pages of graph paper with printed headings for most countries of the world and perhaps some illustrations and a card cover. These can cost less than £1 and are suitable for a schoolchild's first collection.

There are more advanced albums with loose leaves which can have extra pages added as the collection grows. Some of these have printed spaces for every stamp issued by each particular country, others have plain pages which enable the owner to lay out his stamps as he wishes. There are also one-country albums covering part or the whole of the period during which stamps have been issued.

The most expensive productions have transparent pockets on every page, into which stamps are placed without having to use a mounting hinge. For all other albums stamp hinges should be used; these are gummed on one side and the best ones are ready folded and peelable so that they are easy to remove if necessary.

Really keen philatelists like to 'write up' their collections with descriptive information and data on each page. This is done by typing the information on the page before mounting the stamps, or if you are a neat writer using italic or freehand block handwriting. The addition of appropriate information on the album pages makes the collection more interesting and suitable for displaying at exhibitions or meetings.

WHERE TO GET STAMPS

There are stamp shops in towns in many parts of the country, although in recent years more dealers have tended to operate mail order businesses, due to the high cost of renting shops.

There are four specialist monthly stamp magazines which can be obtained from many newsagents. They all contain a wide variety of offers from stamp dealers as well as much interesting editorial on old and new stamps.

Many stamp auctions are held in some of the main towns throughout the country at regular intervals. These are perhaps of more interest to specialist collectors, but there are often some general lots and surplus collections offered for sale. Numerous firms also offer postal auctions and produce illustrated catalogues.

Stamp fairs are a feature of philatelic trading today. These are generally one-day affairs held in local halls where upwards of a dozen dealers will offer a variety of interesting material. These are sometimes advertised locally and are often listed in the stamp magazines.

Large stamp exhibitions are held twice a year in Central London at the Horticultural Halls, Westminster. There are also other periodic shows in London and the provinces.

Thus there are plenty of opportunities to buy stamps and if you are lucky and know a firm which trades with foreign countries you may also be able to get overseas stamps from their mail for a modest payment or gratis.

ACCESSORIES

A variety of accessories are available to help you with your stamp collection. Among the most important are tweezers with rounded or spade ends. These should be used at all times when handling stamps to avoid damaging them.

A folding magnifying glass is well worth having to help close examination of stamps and postmarks. A more sophisticated illuminated glass is also very useful for extensive inspections.

There are several types of watermark detector ranging from a simple black tray with benzine to a battery- or electrically-operated box.

A perforation gauge can be acquired quite cheaply and another useful item is a colour gauge to check shades on stamps.

PUBLICATIONS

A stamp catalogue is an essential reference book for most collectors. Gibbons publish a whole range of these from simplified editions covering the whole world to specialist volumes devoted to one country. A number of other catalogues are also published in the UK and in many overseas territories.

An immense variety of books and leaflets are available covering almost every aspect of philately, starting with simple guides to the hobby and progressing to complicated studies of single issues of Great Britain and of other countries. Some of these can be borrowed from libraries, while others can be purchased from dealers or bookshops.

CLUBS

It is well worth while joining a local stamp club to meet fellow enthusiasts and to participate in meetings which are often held regularly throughout the year. They are generally devoted to various aspects of the hobby and often help to improve one's knowledge about stamps. Many societies also hold regular auction sales of members' duplicates, have a library and organise sales of stamps through circulating packets.

Two well-known national associations are the National Philatelic Society which was founded in 1899 and the British Philatelic Federation. Both have offices at 107 Charterhouse Street, Smithfield, London, EC1, where meetings are held.

As part of their subscription, members of the N.P.S. receive six times per year copies of the Society's journal *Stamp Lover*, which was established in 1908 and has appeared regularly ever since.

GREAT BRITAIN

Issue   PENNY BLACK

Description First adhesive postage stamp. Issued
                 imperforate in sheets of 240, with
                 letters in bottom left and bottom right
                 hand corners, commencing AA in first
                 row, BA in second row etc.

Issue date   6 May 1840.

Printer   Perkins Baker & Petch, London.
                 Process Line engraved. Head of Queen
                 Victoria taken from a drawing for a
                 medal by William Wyon.

Scarcity   About 68 million copies were issued up
                 to February 1841, when the stamp was
                 replaced by the Penny Red. Thus the
                 Penny Black is not rare, but is in great
                 demand throughout the world as the
                 very first postage stamp.

Value   This depends on the condition of each
                 specimen and the plate from which it
                 was printed. Twelve plates were used
                 and number 11 is the most scarce.
                 Stamps were imperforate, and were
                 separated by scissors, so margins vary.

A top quality example having four clear margins and a light Maltese Cross post-mark and printed from one of the most common plates will sell for about £40. Average copies with 3 margins realise around £20.

Issue	## PENNY RED
Description	Successor to the Penny Black. Produced from the same plates initially in the same design, but printed in red to discourage re-use by removing postmark.
Issue date	10 February 1841.
Printer	Perkins Bacon, London. Process Line engraved.
Scarcity	A common stamp – about 2,588 million issued, of which 120 million were later perforated.
Value	Depends on condition and plate from which it was printed. Those printed from plates 1b, 2, 5, 8, 9, 10 and 11 (used also for Penny Black) in good condition are worth around £40 on cover. Unused cost £60 upwards. Plates from 12 upwards are more common and sell from £1 used.

Issue

TWO PENCE BLUE WITH WHITE LINES

Description Similar to the Penny Black, but with white lines above and below the Queen's head. Printed in sheets of 240 in blue ink and imperforate.

Issue date 13 March 1841.

Printer Perkins Bacon, London. Process Line engraved.

Scarcity About 88 million copies printed. Replaced by a perforated version in 1854.

Value Dependent on condition. Clean four-margin copies sell for between £5 and £25.

Issue	# EMBOSSED STAMPS
Description	The first embossed postage stamp had a face value of one shilling as this was the rate for a letter to the USA and also the fee for registered mail.
	The design comprised the head of Queen Victoria and the primary die was engraved by William Wyon who used as his model the profile portrait which he prepared for the City Medal in 1837.
Issue date	11 September 1847.
Printer	The stamps were embossed at Somerset House, but the production was laborious as the presses could only strike one impression at a time and there were twenty impressions to each sheet. Spacing between each imperforate stamp was often uneven, so it is a problem to find fine used specimens with even margins all round.
Scarcity	Difficult to find in good condition mint, despite the fact that well over 5 million copies of the one shilling value were issued.
Value	About £100, in good used condition.

Issue	**HALF-PENNY ROSE RED**
Description	This stamp was produced to prepay postage on printed matter and samples. A tiny format was chosen about two-thirds of the size of a normal stamp. Printed in sheets of 480 in 20 horizontal rows of 24. Lettering in the lower corners of each stamp commencing AA, repeated in reverse in the upper corners.
Issue date	1 October 1870.
Printer	Recess printed by Perkins Bacon & Co on paper watermarked with the words 'half penny'. Fifteen plates were used and the plate number was inscribed within the decorative pattern.
Scarcity	The total number issued was over 1,600 million. Wastage during printing was heavy for over 236 million were spoilt and destroyed.
Value	Used copies of this stamp at about £2 are plentiful but often in poor condition, being either off-centre or heavily postmarked.

Issue	QUEEN VICTORIA £5 STAMP
Description	This was the highest value stamp issued by Great Britain for over a century. The word 'Postage' appears above the Queen's head and beneath the value in words. The figure £5 is boldly placed to left and right of the portrait and in the bottom corners are positional letters commencing AA for the first stamp on the sheet and finishing with DN on the last stamp in the fourth row.
Issue date	21 March 1882.
Printer	Printed in sheets of 56 stamps on paper watermarked with large anchors, by De La Rue. Perforation 14. Only one plate was used and the figure 1 appears in the top left and top right hand corners.
Scarcity	Nearly a quarter of a million £5 stamps were issued. A low figure for a British production.
Value	Average price for a good used specimen is around £650 if printed on white paper and approximately £1,000 if printed on the more scarce blued paper.

Issue	# KING EDWARD VII DEFINITIVES
Description	A series of definitive stamps for the reign of King Edward VII was issued in 1902 in values ranging from $\frac{1}{2}$d to 9d. Other values up to £1 appeared at various later dates. The low values were all based on the Queen Victoria Jubilee set which was issued 1887–1892, but with the new King's head as the main feature.
Issue date	1 January 1902 and later.
Printer	The initial printings were by De La Rue, but at later dates both Harrison & Sons Ltd and Somerset House produced some of the stamps. These stamps are renowned for the great variety of shades which can be found on most values which are often difficult to identify by inexperienced collectors. Designed by E. Fuchs. Perforation 14×14.
Scarcity	The one shilling value which is illustrated sold over 125 million copies.
Value	In mint condition the one shilling stamp is worth about £50.

Issue	## 1d RED & 1½d BROWN TO COMMEMORATE THE BRITISH EMPIRE EXHIBITION, WEMBLEY 1924
Description	These were the first commemorative stamps issued by the British Post Office and were larger than the current definitive range. The stamps depict the British Lion, with the head of King George V inset.
Issue date	23 April 1924.
Printer	Recess printed by Waterlow & Sons Ltd on paper watermarked Multiple Crown GvR. Engraved by J. A. C. Harrison. Designer Harold Nelson. Each sheet of stamps comprised 120 stamps. Perforation 14. The exhibition closed on 1 November 1924, but opened again on 9 May 1925 when the stamps were re-issued with the date changed to 1925.
Scarcity	Exact quantity printed of these two pairs of stamps is believed to be 17 million. Over 13 million of the 1924

issue were sold and about 3.5 million of the 1925 pair.

Value   The 1924 issue is less scarce and sells for about £12 mint, whereas the 1925 pair are worth around £35.

Issue   £1 POSTAL UNION CONGRESS 1929

Description   To celebrate the ninth congress of the Universal Postal Congress which was held in London in May 1929, the Post Office decided to issue a set of five values – ½d., 1d., 1½d., 2½d. and £1. The decision to produce a £1 value was because the Post Office wanted to present all delegates to the conference with a set of the special stamps and it was considered desirable that the gift should have a worthwhile value. In fact the £1 value did have quite considerable commercial use on heavy, insured and airmail packages.

Issue date   10 May 1929.

Printer   Recess printed by Bradbury Wilkinson & Co Ltd from their own plates, on watermarked paper showing the letters GvR surmounted by a crown.
Designed by Harold Nelson.
The stamp, perforated 12, was the largest size chosen at that date and has rarely been exceeded since. Printed in sheets of 20, the stamp remained on sale at some post offices for about ten years.

Scarcity   One of the rarest twentieth-century Great Britain stamps, with about 61,000 copies sold.

Value   About £500 for a mint copy.

Issue   KING GEORGE V SILVER JUBILEE 2½d

Description   To commemorate the Silver Jubilee of the reign of King George V a set of four stamps comprised ½d. green, 1d. red,

1½d. brown and 2½d. blue was produced. Three different multipositives were used, causing a variation in the shading in the value panel on the three lowest values.

Issue date   7 May 1935.

Printer   For the first time photogravure process was used for printing commemoratives and the work was undertaken by Harrison & Sons Ltd. Perforation 15 × 14. Watermark multiple crown block cypher. Printing was on long reels of paper which were then cut into sheets of 120 stamps each. Designer Barnett Freedman.

Scarcity   The Jubilee set is quite common as a total of about 14 million of the highest value were sold and many more of the other stamps. However three sheets were issued in error printed in a colour trial, namely Prussian blue, and these are scarce.

Value   The standard 2½d. stamp sells for about £2. The Prussian blue variation can realise £2,000.

Issue	## KING EDWARD VIII DEFINITIVES
Description	The brief reign of Edward VIII, which lasted less than a year, meant that there was only time to issue stamps of the four lowest values namely ½d., 1d., 1½d. and 2½d. These were noteworthy for the simplicity of the design which comprised the head of the King from a photograph by Hugh Cecil, with the word 'Postage' at the bottom, the value figure was in the top right hand corner and a crown in the top left corner.
Issue date	1 September 1936. The issue was withdrawn on 29 July 1937, but booklets were still on sale up to the end of that year.
Printer	Printed photogravure by Harrison & Sons Ltd in sheets of 240 stamps on paper watermarked E8R with crown over. Perforation 15 × 14. The design was based on an unsolicited suggestion by H. J. Brown, a seventeen-year-old member of the Exeter and Torquay Philatelic Society.

Scarcity　32 million stamps were sold of the highest value and much higher quantities of the other three values, so supplies are plentiful both mint and used.

Value　A mint set of four stamps can be purchased for less than £1.

Issue

1937 CORONATION OF KING GEORGE VI

Description　A single stamp was issued for this event. The value was 1½d., which was the inland postage rate for a letter at the time. The stamp was printed in a single colour (deep brown) and was double the size of the normal definitive low value. It was designed by Edmund Dulac and showed portraits of the King and Queen Elizabeth. The words 'Postage' and 'Revenue' were incorporated across the top and under the portraits was the date 12 May 1937, with the value 1½d. in the left and right hand corners. A crown, royal cypher and other embellishments were also incorporated.

Issue date   13 May 1937 (the day after the
             Coronation ceremony, which was a
             public holiday).

Printer   The photogravure process was used by
             Harrison & Sons Ltd. The stamps were
             printed in sheets of 120 on paper
             watermarked with the royal cypher
             (GviR) and perforated 15×14.

Scarcity   Over 388 million stamps were sold so
             the stamp is common, both mint and
             used.

Value   These stamps can be purchased for a
             few pence, but good quality illustrated
             first day covers are more difficult to find
             and may realise £10 or more.

Issue   GERMAN WAR
             PROPAGANDA ISSUES

Description During the Second World War both
             sides employed many propaganda
             stunts. In reply to bogus German
             stamps showing the portrait of
             Himmler in place of Hitler, which were
             dropped by allied aircraft over
             Germany in 1943, the Nazis produced
             their own philatelic propaganda. This

comprised replicas of the Great Britain 1½d. Coronation stamp of 1937 with the portrait of Queen Elizabeth replaced by one of Stalin.

The ½d. Jubilee stamp of 1935 was also forged with a picture of Stalin in place of King George V and the inscription altered to 'This War is a Jewish War'.

Issue date   Believed to be 1944.

Printer   The work appears to have been undertaken in a concentration camp by specialist staff who forged currency, passports and documents for overseas agents and spies.

Scarcity   It is not known how many of these stamps were printed, but they do not now come on the market in the UK very often.

Value   Current market price approximately £70 each.

Issue   **1940 STAMP CENTENARY**

Description   It was intended to hold an international stamp exhibition in 1940 at Earls

Court, London, to celebrate the
centenary of the first adhesive postage
stamp, namely the Penny Black. The
outbreak of the war against Germany
in September 1939 caused these plans to
be cancelled, but the Post Office
decided to issue six stamps to mark the
centenary. In addition a special
exhibition at Lancaster House,
London, in aid of the Lord Mayor's
Red Cross and St John Fund, was
hurriedly organised for 6–14 May.
The centenary set comprised values at
half-penny steps from ½d. to 3d.

Issue date 6 May 1940.

Printer Printed by Harrison & Sons Ltd on
paper watermarked multiple crown
GviR. Designer H. L. Palmer.
Perforated 14.5×14.

Scarcity The stamps were on sale for about two
months and the quantities sold were
approximately 22 million of the highest
value (3d.) and 312 million of the most
commonly used value (2½d.).

Value A complete set of six mint sells for
about £3.

Issue

1946 VICTORY

Description

To commemorate victory in the Second World War a pair of double size stamps appeared in the summer of 1946. There were two values 2½d. ultramarine and 3d. violet, each bearing the head of King George VI with a crown above and symbols of peace and reconstruction. The words 'postage' and 'revenue' appeared left and right respectively on both designs.
The lower value was designed by H. L. Palmer, an artist of the printers Harrison & Sons Ltd, and the other was the work of Reynolds Stone.

Issue date

11 June 1946.

Printer

Printed on paper watermarked GviR by Harrisons.

Scarcity

Quantity issued was nearly 308 million of the lower value and over 43 million for 3d. stamp.

Value

These two stamps are still available in considerable quantities and sell for about 20p the pair mint.

Issue	ROYAL SILVER WEDDING 1948
Description	In recognition of the 25th anniversary of the wedding of King George VI and Queen Elizabeth a low value and a high value stamp were issued. The denominations being 2½d. which was the standard inland letter rate and £1 which was used mainly for heavier air-mail letters. The stamps were dignified and simple in design and based on photographs of the King and Queen taken by Dorothy Wilding.
Issue date	26 April 1948.
Printer	Harrison & Sons Ltd. Designers G. Knipe and Joan Hassall. Perforation 15 × 14. Printed in sheets of 20.
Scarcity	147.5 million copies of the low value were sold, but the £1 value only sold 419,600 copies.
Value	The low value is available in considerable quantities and can be acquired for a few pence both mint and used. The £1 stamp in mint condition costs about £20.

Issue	LIBERATION OF THE CHANNEL ISLANDS
Description	The Channel Islands, which lie off the coast of Northern France near Cherbourg, were the only part of the United Kingdom to be occupied by Germany during the Second World War. To mark the third anniversary of their liberation in 1945, the British Post Office issued a pair of stamps intended mainly for use in the islands, but they were also on sale at eight Head Post Offices in Great Britain and were valid for use throughout the UK. The two stamps depicted islanders gathering Vraic (a local seaweed used as an agricultural fertiliser), with two different scenes.
Issue date	10 May 1948.
Printer	Printed by Harrison & Sons Ltd. Designer of the 1d. stamp was J. R. R. Stobie. The 2½d. value was illustrated from a drawing by E. Blampied. Perforation 15 × 14.
Scarcity	Nearly 6 million copies of the 1d. were sold and 5.4 million of the higher value.
Value	The mint stamps sell for about 25p.

Issue	## OLYMPIC GAMES 1948
Description	The first post-war Olympic Games were held at Wembley Stadium, London, in the summer of 1948 and a set of four stamps was issued.
Issue date	29 July 1948
Printer	Paper watermarked multiple crown GviR was used by Harrison & Sons Ltd who printed the stamps by photogravure.
	These were designed by four different artists.
	The two illustrated were the work of Stanley D. Scott (6d. bright purple – showing the well-known Olympic Circle of five intertwined rings with floral decoration either side) and Edmund Dulac (1s. brown – depicting the allegorical image 'Winged Victory' above a globe of the earth). The other designers were Percy Metcalfe ($2\frac{1}{2}$d.) and Abram Games (3d.).
	Perforation 15×14. 120 stamps per sheet.
Scarcity	A popular set with thematic collectors. Sales (approximately) $2\frac{1}{2}$d. – 155 million; 3d. – 32 million; 6d. – 24 million; 1s. – 32 million.
Value	About £1 for a mint set.

Issue

UNIVERSAL POSTAL UNION 75th ANNIVERSARY

Description To secure international co-operation in the carriage of mail the Universal Postal Union was founded in 1874 by H. von Stephan, the German Postmaster General at the time. To mark the 75th anniversary of this significant event, many countries in various parts of the world issued special stamps. The British authorities decided to produce a set of four stamps in the same values and colours as the Olympic games series.

Issue date 10 October 1949.

Printer Paper watermarked multiple crown GviR was used by Harrison. Perforation 15×14. Printed in sheets of 120. The designers were Mary Adshead ($2\frac{1}{2}$d.), P. Metcalfe (3d.), H. Fleury (6d.) and the Hon. G. Bellew (1s.).

Scarcity Quantities sold were about 135 million for $2\frac{1}{2}$d. value, 16 million for the 3d., 11 million of the 6d. and a similar quantity of the 1s. stamp.

Value The mint set retails for around £1.50.

Issue

FESTIVAL OF BRITAIN 1951

Description   The first great event in London to promote Britain as a country and an industrial nation after the Second World War was the Festival of Britain, held on the south bank of the River Thames, adjacent to Waterloo station, London. Two low value stamps were issued.
A portrait of King George VI also appears on both stamps and this was the last issue of his reign, for he died on 6 February 1952.

Issue date   3 May 1951.

Printer   Paper watermarked multiple crown GviR was used. Perforation 15 × 14. Printed in sheets of 120 by Harrison & Sons Ltd. The designers were E. Dulac (2½d.) and A. Games (4d.).

Scarcity   Quantity sold:- about 260 million of the low value and 22 million of the 4d.

Value   The illustrated first day cover at about £10 is worth considerably more than the mint set which sells for about 30p.

REIGN OF
QUEEN ELIZABETH II

Over 250 sets of commemorative stamps plus more than one hundred definitive stamps have been issued by the British Post Office over the past four decades during the reign of Queen Elizabeth II. On the following pages the author has selected a variety of issues to try and give a representative selection of the more interesting items.

Issue	CORONATION OF QUEEN ELIZABETH II
Description	A set of four stamps was produced for this very important event and they have been proclaimed as among the best looking stamps issued during the first decade of the reign.

Illustrated is the 1s.3d. value (green) a dignified design by Edmund Dulac showing a half length, full face portrait of the Queen in Coronation robes. The other stamps all include a three-quarter face portrait from a photograph by Dorothy Wilding, with a framework of Coronation emblems and ornamentation.

Issue date   3 June 1953.

Printer   Printed photogravure by Harrison on paper watermarked E2R surmounted by a Tudor crown. E. G. Fuller designed the 2½d. (red), Michael Goaman the 4d. (blue), E. Dulac the 1s.3d. (green) and M. C. Farrar-Bell the 1s.6d. (blue). Perforation 15 × 14. Sheets of 120 stamps.

Scarcity   As less then 6 million copies of the top value were sold, the set is comparatively rare compared with other QE II commemoratives.

Value   The full set costs about £10, in mint condition.

Issue	**WORLD SCOUT JAMBOREE JUBILEE**
Description	The Jamboree Jubilee celebrated the 50th anniversary of the founding of the Boy Scout movement and was held at Sutton Coldfield, Warwickshire. Three stamps were issued with Scouting associations and the top value depicted a globe with a compass, indicative of the movement's worldwide associations.
Issue date	1 August 1957.
Printer	Harrison & Sons Ltd. Designers Mary Adshead (2½d.), Pat Keely (4d.) and W. H. Brown (1s.3d.). Perforated 15 × 14. Printed in sheets of 120.
Scarcity	Sales of the low value were over 133 million, the middle value sold about 9 million and the 1s.3d. only 3.8 million. Rolls of stamps were prepared to affix stamps to over 60,000 first day covers.
Value	The mint set of three sells for about £4.

Issue	CONFERENCE OF CEPT
Description	The second anniversary Conference of the European Postal and Telecommunications Administration was held at Torquay, Devon, in September 1961 and was marked by the issue of three stamps showing the CEPT emblem and other adornments. This set was noteworthy as it was the first Great Britain stamps to be printed in three colours.
Issue date	18 September 1961.
Printer	Printed on chalk surfaced paper by Harrison & Sons Ltd in sheets of 120. Designer Michael Goaman. Perforation 15 × 14.
Scarcity	Over 47 million copies were sold of the 2d. value, 7.6 million of the 4d. stamp and about 5.4 million of the 10d. stamp.
Value	The selling price of this mint set of three stamps is around 30p.

Issue

CENTENARY OF POST OFFICE SAVINGS BANK

Description Thrift as a theme was very much in evidence on a set of three stamps to mark this important centenary. The plant thrift, whose botanical name is *Armeria maritima*, appears on the 2½d. and 1s.6d. stamps. It is a small perennial of the sea-lavender family which is found along the coasts of Britain and in Europe. The flowers are almost everlasting and are perhaps symbolic of economy of expenditure.

Issue date 28 August 1961.

Printer Printed on chalk surfaced paper by Harrison & Sons Ltd. Designed by P. Gauld (2½d.) and Michael Goaman (3d. and 1s.6d). Perforation 14 × 15 or 15 × 14. Printed in sheets of 120.

Scarcity The 3d. value sold most copies at about 114 million. Sales of the low value were 24.7 million and the high value approximately 7.5 million.

Value The mint set of three sells for about £1.50.

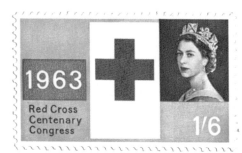

Issue	RED CROSS CENTENARY CONGRESS
Description	Held in Geneva, Switzerland on 2 September the congress celebrated the centenary of the establishment of the worldwide renowned Red Cross organisation. Their familiar insignia formed a prominent feature on each of the three stamps.
Issue date	15 August 1963.
Printer	Printed by Harrison & Sons Ltd on chalk surfaced paper. Designer H. Bartram. Perforation 15 × 14. Sheets of 120 stamps.
Scarcity	The 3d. stamp sold 167 million copies. The 1s.3d. and 1s.6d. values reached about 8 million copies each.
Value	The mint set of three values sells for around £3.50.

Issue	**INTERNATIONAL LIFEBOAT CONFERENCE**
Description	The ninth International Lifeboat Conference was held at Edinburgh in June 1963. These events are held in various locations every four years and the Post Office decided to issue three stamps to record the event in Scotland which took place between 3–5 June. Rescue at sea, lifeboats and lifeboat-men were depicted.
Issue date	31 May 1963.
Printer	Printed on chalk surface paper by Harrison & Sons Ltd. Designer David Gentleman. Perforation 15 × 14. Printed in sheets of 120.
Scarcity	Nearly 86 million copies of the 2½d. value were sold, and about 8 million each of the 4d. and 1s.6d.
Value	The mint set of three values sells for around £3.

Issue   ## SHAKESPEARE FESTIVAL

Description   A set of five stamps was issued to commemorate the four hundredth anniversary of William Shakespeare's birth, (1564–1616), considered to be England's greatest poet and dramatist. Scenes from several of his plays are depicted on the stamps including Hamlet contemplating Yorick's skull on the 2s.6d. design. For the first time the Post Office produced presentation packs of this issue containing a set of the stamps and information about the issue.

Issue date   23 April 1964.

Printer   Recess printed by Bradbury Wilkinson. Designers Christopher and Robin Ironside.
Perforation 15 × 14 except the high value which is 11 × 12. Printed in sheets of 120, except the 2s.6d. which was in sheets of 40.

Scarcity   Only about 3.6 million copies of the high value were sold. The others ranged from over 133 million of the 3d. stamp,

19 million of the 6d. value and around 8 million each of the 1s.3d. and 1s.6d. stamps.

Value   The mint set sells for about £2.50.

Issue   # CENTENARY OF SALVATION ARMY

Description   The Salvation Army was formed in 1865 by William Booth, a Methodist minister.
This religious organisation operated on semi-military lines, but with the aim of rescuing the delinquent poor, the destitute and alcoholics and introducing them to Christianity. The Army is still famous for its welfare work, brass bands and efforts to preach the Gospel in the streets. It now operates on a worldwide basis.
The two stamps issued to mark the centenary show bandsmen and the Salvation Army banner (3d.) and three Salvationists in uniform (1s.6d.).

Issue date   9 August 1965.

Printer	Printed on chalk surface paper in sheets of 120 by Harrison & Sons Ltd. M. C. Farrar-Bell designed the lower value and G. Trenaman the higher value. Perforation 15 × 14.
Scarcity	Over 58 million copies of the 3d. value were issued and less than 6 million of the 1s.6d.
Value	The mint pair sell for about £1.

Issue	## 25th ANNIVERSARY BATTLE OF BRITAIN 1965
Description	Eight stamps were issued for this event, each with a different illustration. Six of these bore the value 4d. and were produced se-tenant in blocks of 3 × 2. The other values were 9d. and 1s.3d. The 4d. stamp illustrated depicted Hurricane aircraft of the RAF over the wreck of a German DO-17z2 bomber.
Issue date	13 September 1965.

| **Printer** | Printed in sheets of 120 by Harrison & Sons Ltd. Designed by David Gentleman and Rosalind Dease, except for the 9d. value which was undertaken by A. Restall. The perforation was 15 × 14 and a chalk surface paper was used. |

Printer　Printed in sheets of 120 by Harrison & Sons Ltd. Designed by David Gentleman and Rosalind Dease, except for the 9d. value which was undertaken by A. Restall. The perforation was 15 × 14 and a chalk surface paper was used.

Scarcity　About 115 million copies of the 4d. values were issued and over 7 million each of the two higher values. A presentation pack of this set sold about 28,500 copies.

Value　The set of eight stamps in mint condition sells for around £5, but the presentation pack realises several times this figure as the quantity issued was quite low.

Issue　# OPENING OF THE POST OFFICE TOWER

Description　The Post Office Tower was built in the centre of London, principally to provide more long distance telephone circuits and TV channels. It cost £2.5

million to construct and is 580 feet
high. It is surmounted by a 40 foot high
trellis mast supporting radar aerials
designed to help short range weather
forecasting.

Near the top of the mast an observation
gallery and public revolving restaurant
were incorporated, but these facilities
were subsequently withdrawn for
security reasons. The two stamps
illustrate the Tower and Georgian
buildings (3d. value), and the Tower
and 'Nash' Terrace, Regent's Park,
which can be seen from the summit.

Issue date   8 October 1965.

Printer   Printed on chalk surfaced paper. For
the first time, on British stamps, the
name of the printer – Harrison & Sons
Ltd – and the designer – Clive Abbott –
were incorporated in the design.
Perforation 14×15 on the 3d. value
and 15×14 on the 1s.3d. stamp.

Scarcity   Over 55 million copies of the lower
value and 6.8 million of the higher
value were sold.

Value   About 50p for the pair mint.

Issue	LANDSCAPES
Description	This was the first special issue not devoted to a current event or important anniversary and to have a cameo portrait of the Queen. The four values had illustrations of different countries, namely England, Northern Ireland, Wales and Scotland. A lovely rural view near Hassocks in Sussex appeared on the 4d. value, the hills of Antrim were illustrated on the 6d. stamp, historic Harlech Castle was on the 1s.3d. stamp and the top value (1s.6d.) showed a dramatic view of the Cairngorm mountains.
Issue date	2 May 1966.
Printer	The photogravure process was used by Harrison & Sons Ltd. to produce this set. Printed on chalk surfaced paper, the stamps were designed by Leonard Rosoman and the Queen's head reproduction was adapted by David Gentleman from coinage.
Scarcity	Sales were over 91 million of the 4d., nearly 14 million for the 6d. and about 6.5 million each of the two top values.
Value	The set of four mint sells for under £1.

Issue	WORLD CUP FOOTBALL COMPETITION
Description	A set of three stamps was issued for the World Cup Football competition held at Wembley and elsewhere in England and these were the first British stamps featuring sport. When England was victorious in the final on 31 July, it was decided to produce a modified version of the 4d. value incorporating the words 'England Winners' across the top.
Issue date	1 June 1966 for the set of three. 18 August 1966 for the 'England Winners' 4d.
Printer	Printed in sheets of 120 in five colours by Harrison & Sons Ltd. Designed by David Gentleman (4d.), William Kempster (6d.) and David Caplan (1s.3d.). Perforation 14 × 15.
Scarcity	146 million copies of the 4d. were sold, over 20 million of the 6d. and more than 8 million of the 1s.3d. stamp.
Value	The mint set is still available in considerable quantities at about 50p. The 'winners' single value fetches about 15p.

BLUE TIT
J NORRIS WOOD
HARRISON AND SONS LTD
4d

Issue	## BRITISH BIRDS 1966
Description	These were the first British stamps to be printed in eight colours. They were produced in se-tenant blocks of four different designs showing typical English birds as follows:- a blackbird, European robin, blue tit and black-headed gull. All were of the same value – 4d.
Issue date	8 August 1966
Printer	Printed in sheets of 120 (i.e. 30 blocks of four) by Harrison & Sons Ltd. Designer J. Norris Wood. Perforation 15 × 14.
Scarcity	About 102 million stamps were sold.
Value	A set of four mint costs about 50p. A number of errors with certain colours missing have been discovered. Some of these are considered to be worth £100 or more.

Issue	**900th ANNIVERSARY BATTLE OF HASTINGS**
Description	The best known date in English History – 1066 – was celebrated 900 years later with a set of eight stamps showing artists' impressions of scenes from the Bayeaux Tapestry of the Battle of Hastings when King Harold was defeated by William the Conqueror and his Norman horsemen. There were six versions of the 4d. value all with different battle scenes and these were issued se-tenant in strips of six within sheets of 120 stamps. The 6d. showed a Norman ship and the 1s.3d. value was illustrated with Norman horsemen attacking King Harold's troops. Both had a silhouette of the Queen's head die-stamped in gold and the higher value was larger than normal for a commemorative.
Issue date	14 October 1966.
Printer	Printed on chalk surface paper by Harrison & Sons Ltd. Designed by David Gentleman.

Scarcity   The 4d. value sold over 105 million copies, 6d. value nearly 15 million and the top value over 7 million.

Value   Set of eight mint stamps about £1. A number of colour omissions are known, which fetch premium prices.

Issue

EUROPEAN FREE TRADE ASSOCIATION

Description   A pair of stamps was issued to mark the establishment of the first free trade area in the world which came into being on 31 December 1966 between seven countries namely Austria, Denmark, Norway, Portugal, Sweden, Switzerland and the United Kingdom, plus Finland as an associate member. The 9d. value illustrates sea freight with a merchant ship being loaded and bearing the flags of the member countries. The 1s.6d. stamp depicts air freight with a cargo plane being loaded and the flags.

Issue date   20 February 1967.

Printer	Printed photogravure in eight and nine colours respectively by Harrison & Sons Ltd. in sheets of 120. Designed by Clive Abbott.
Scarcity	About 11 million copies of each stamp were sold.
Value	Although sales of this pair were lower than for many other contemporary commemoratives, the retail price is only about 20p.

Issue	CHRISTMAS 1967
Description	Continuing the tradition commenced in the previous year a special issue of stamps was issued in 1967 to commemorate Christmas. The designs illustrate classical paintings as follows: 3d. – *Adoration of the Shepherds* ascribed to the School of Seville, 4d. – *Madonna and Child* by Murillo, 1s.6d. – *The Adoration of the Shepherds* by Louis Le Nain.

The original painting of the Madonna and child is housed in the Rijks Museum at Amsterdam and the other two are in the National Gallery, London. The Queen's head and the value were printed in gold.
These stamps offered philatelists the opportunity of acquiring reproductions of old masters worth millions of pounds for a very nominal sum.

Issue date 4d. – 18 October, other values – 27 November 1967.

Printer As from this issue all British commemoratives were printed on unwatermarked paper. Once again Harrisons were responsible for the printing and chalk surfaced paper was used. The two lower values comprised 120 stamps per sheet and the high value had 60 stamps on each sheet.

Scarcity For the Christmas rush immense quantities were printed. Sales were in excess of 270 million for the 3d., nearly 288 million for the middle value and almost 18 million of the 1s.6d. were purchased.

Value There are plentiful supplies of this issue still available at around 20p for the mint trio.

Issue   # BRITISH DISCOVERY & INVENTION

Description Radar was of immense importance to the war effort in 1939–1945 and Britain was first in the world with an efficient radar system through pioneer Robert Watson-Watt. In more recent years development of the system still further has ensured extra safety in the air and at sea. A radar screen is shown on the 4d. value. Other inventions commemorated on this set were television (1s.9d. stamp), jet engine (1s.6d.) and penicillin (1s.).

Issue date 19 September 1967.

Printer   Printer Harrison & Sons Ltd gained the Queen's Award for Industry in 1967 having produced 46 commemorative issues of stamps, including this set, since 1935 by photogravure. The designers were Clive Abbott for the two low values, Richard Negus and Philip Sharland for the other stamp. Printed in sheets of 120. Perforation 14 × 15.

Scarcity   104 million copies were sold of the 4d., about 10 million of the middle values and over 7 million of the 1s.9d. stamp.

Value   Set of four mint approximately 30p.

Issue   # BRITISH ANNIVERSARIES – VOTES FOR WOMEN

Description   The 9d. value in this set pictured a statue of Mrs Emmeline Pankhurst and was inscribed 'Votes for Women 1918–1968'. It was in 1918 that a registration bill was passed which contained a clause giving women the right to vote in elections providing they were thirty years old, were householders or married to householders. This concession was only achieved after a lengthy campaign by the Suffragettes under Mrs Pankhurst. Their protests included marches through London, chaining themselves to important public buildings and one member was killed through throwing herself in front of the

King's horse racing in the Derby in 1914.

Other stamps in this series comprised:- 4d. – centenary of the T.U.C., 1s. – Sopwith Camel and Lightning Fighters RAF 1918–1968 and 1s.9d. – bi-centenary of Capt. Cook's first voyage of discovery, 1768 in the *Endeavour*.

Issue date   29 May 1968.

Printer   Harrison. 120 stamps per sheet. Designers: 4d. – David Gentleman, others – Clive Abbott. Perforation 15×14.

Scarcity   The low value sold nearly 98 million copies. Sales were in excess of 9 million for the two middle values and around 6 million for the top value.

Value   The set can be bought for about 40p.

Issue   # BRITISH PAINTINGS

Description   The printers made photographs of four well known British paintings for these stamps, as follows:-

4d. stamp – *Queen Elizabeth I* by an unknown artist.
1s. – '*Pinkie*' by Sir Thomas Lawrence.
1s.6d. – *Ruins of St Mary Le Port* by John Piper.
1s.9d. – *The Hay Wain*, one of John Constable's best known landscapes.

Issue date   12 August 1968.

Printer   Photogravure by Harrison & Sons Ltd. Perforated 15 × 14 for the top value and 14 × 15 for the other stamps. Printed in sheets of 60 stamps.

Scarcity   Over 185 million copies of the low value were sold. Figures for the other stamps were nearly 18 million for the 1s. stamp, nearly 9 million for the 1s.6d. value and 5.7 million for the top value.

Value   About 40p for the mint set.

RMS Mauretania

RMS Queen Elizabeth 2

Issue   BRITISH SHIPS

Description   As a tribute to British seamen and shipbuilders, the Post Office produced six stamps early in 1969. These showed

five well known ships from the past and
the latest triumph of British nautical
enterprise the RMS *Queen Elizabeth 2*,
(5d. value) the transatlantic liner of
67,000 tons which sailed on her maiden
voyage on 2 May 1969. The renowned
liner *Mauretania* one of the most
famous North Atlantic ships during the
first part of this century appeared on
the 1s. value. Her maiden voyage was
in 1907. Brunel's first iron-clad
steamship SS *Great Britain* appears on
the 1s. value. While the 9d. stamp was
issued in se-tenant strips of three
showing an Elizabethan galleon, an
East Indiaman and the tea-clipper
Cutty Sark.

Issue date 15 January 1969.

Printer Harrison printed the 5d. value in sheets
of 72 because of its abnormally wide
format, for the 9d. value se-tenant
strips of three throughout the sheets of
120 stamps was the arrangement and
the 1s. value was produced in se-tenant
pairs in sheets of 80 stamps. The
designer was David Gentleman.
Perforation 15 × 14.

Scarcity 67 million of the QE2 stamp were sold.
More than 14 million of the 9d and 10.7
million of the 1s. stamp.

Value The six values can be bought for less
than £1.

Issue

FIRST FLIGHT OF CONCORDE

Description   The first flight of Concorde the unique
supersonic airliner, which was a joint
British and French enterprise, was
commemorated with the issue of three
stamps which emphasised the unusual
lines of the aircraft. An artist's
impression of Concorde in flight
appeared on the 4d. stamp. The 9d.
and 1s.6d. values depicted plan and
elevation views, plus the aircraft's nose
and tail.

Issue date   3 March 1969.

Printer   Harrison on chalk surfaced paper.
Perforation 15 × 14. The lowest value
design was the joint work of Michael
and Sylvia Goaman.
David Gentleman was responsible for
the design of the other two stamps.

Scarcity   Sales of the 4d. value were about 91
million. The other two values sold
about 9 million each.

Value   These sets can be bought for about 20p
each.

Issue

INVESTITURE OF THE PRINCE OF WALES

Description In the summer of 1969 the Queen held
the investiture of her eldest son, Prince
Charles as Prince of Wales at
Caernarvon in North Wales. This
historic ceremony dates back to 1284
when King Edward I presented his son
to the nation at Caernarvon.
A set of five stamps were issued for the
twentieth-century event comprising a
triptych of the 5d. value showing three
buildings which played a prominent
part in the ceremony namely the King's
Gate, the Eagle Tower and Queen
Eleanor's Gate, all part of Caernarvon
Castle.
The Celtic Cross, Margam Abbey,
appeared on the 9d. stamp and a
portrait of HRH The Prince of Wales
from a photograph by G. Argent was
used on the top value (1s.), designed by
David Gentleman.

Issue date   1 July 1969.

Printer   The 5d. values printed in se-tenant strips of three by Harrison were in sheets of 72. The other two values were issued in sheets of 60.

Scarcity   Nearly 100 million of the 5d. value were sold. The other values sold about 13 million each.

Value   The mint set sells for about 40p.

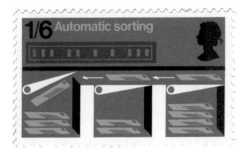

Issue   POST OFFICE TECHNOLOGY

Description   In 1969 the Post Office was dealing with about 36 million letters and parcels plus 29 million telephone calls every day, in addition to providing savings and money facilities, also services for various Government departments.
To achieve all these tasks it was necessary to introduce the latest technology.
The four stamps in this set record mechanisation with automatic sorting of mail (1s.6d. stamp), Pulse code modulation for the telephone system (1s. value), International subscriber

dialling (9d. stamp) and National Giro, the newly introduced banking system (5d. value).

Issue date   1 October 1969.

Printer   Thomas de la Rue & Co Ltd printed this issue in 'Delacryl' an improved offset lithographic technique. Stamps designed by David Gentleman. Perforation 13.5 × 14. Printed in sheets of 120.

Scarcity   Over 72 million copies were sold of the low value. The others sold between 8 and 10 million copies.

Value   The four stamps mint sell for around 50p.

Issue   # BRITISH RURAL ARCHITECTURE

Description   Homes in villages throughout the British Isles were often built of local materials in the old days and this set of four stamps illustrates four methods of construction.

Fife harling, a technique of rendering the surface with a light-coloured cement wash appears on the 5d. value. Cotswold limestone is illustrated on the 9d. stamp. The other two values are devoted to Welsh stucco (1s.) and Ulster thatch (1s.6d. value).

Issue date　11 February 1970.

Printer　Photogravure by Harrison & Sons Ltd. Designer David Gentleman for low value and S. Robinson for 1s. and 1s.6d. Perforation 15×14. Printed in sheets of 120 for the two low values and sheets of 60 stamps for the others.

Scarcity　About 81 million low value stamps were sold, around 10 and 11 million of each of the two middle values and nearly 9 million for the 1s.6d.

Value　This set sells for around 40p, mint.

Issue　# GENERAL ANNIVERSARIES 1970

Description　One of the most interesting stamps (9d.) in this set of five reminds us of the

150th anniversary of the birth of nurse
and hospital reformer Florence
Nightingale. For her work among the
sick she was awarded the Order of
Merit in 1907 and allowed the Freedom
of the City of London.
Other events in the set comprise 600th
anniversary of the Declaration of
Arbroath (5d.), 75th anniversary of the
International Co-operative Alliance
(1s.), Pilgrim Fathers and the
Mayflower (1s.6d.) and 150th birthday
of the Royal Astronomical Society
(1s.9d.).

Issue date   1 April 1970.

Printer   Harrison & Sons Ltd by photogravure.
Designer Fritz Wegner for the 5d., 9d.
and 1s.6d., balance by Marjorie
Saynor. Perforation 15×14.
Printed in sheets of 120.

Scarcity   Over 71 million of the low value were
sold. About 6 million of the top value
and 10 million to 11 million of the
others.

Value   The mint set costs about 50p.

Issue

LITERARY ANNIVERSARIES

Description   Four out of the five stamps in this set were devoted to recording the centenary of the death of Charles Dickens, the author. These stamps all having a face value of 5d. were issued se-tenant in blocks of four. They illustrated etchings from some of the best-known novels as follows:-
Pickwick and Sam Weller by Phiz (Hablot Knight Brown) from *Pickwick Papers*; *Restoration of Mutual Confidence between Mr & Mrs Micawber* (also by Phiz) from the *Personal History of David Copperfield* and *I Make Myself Known to my Aunt* – David Copperfield and Betsy Trotwood; *Oliver Twist asking for more* by George Cruickshank from *Oliver Twist*.
The fifth stamp, a 1s.6d. value, commemorated the centenary of the birth of William Wordsworth (1770–1850) and showed a view of Grasmere from an engraving by J. Farrington.

Issue date   3 June 1970.

Printer	Printed on chalk surfaced paper by Harrison & Sons Ltd. Designed by Rosalind Dease. Perforated 14 × 15.
Scarcity	Over 80 million were sold of the 5d. values and nearly 11 million of the top value.
Value	Around 50p is the current market value of the mint set.

Issue	**NINTH BRITISH COMMONWEALTH GAMES**
Description	First held in Ontario, Canada in 1930, these Games were considered to be second only to the Olympics. The ninth event took place in Edinburgh between 16 and 25 July 1970 and over forty member countries of the British Commonwealth Games Federation took part. Three stamps were issued depicting track events (5d.), swimming (1s.6d.) and cycling (1s.9d.).

Issue date 15 July 1970.

Printer Thomas de la Rue used the 'Delacryl' offset lithographic process to produce this set.
Designer J. Andrew Restall.
Perforation 13.5 × 14. Printed in sheets of 120.

Scarcity Sales were about 75 million of 5d. stamp, 11 million of 1s.6d. and 6 million for 1s.9d.

Value About 50p for the mint set of three.

1840 first engraved issue

1855 first surface printed issue

Issue # PHILYMPIA '70 STAMP EXHIBITION

Description An excellent set of three stamps was issued for this important philatelic event.
International exhibitions such as this one are only held once every ten years in England. The location chosen was part of the Olympia complex, one of the best-known public showplaces in central London.

Early stamps printed by three different processes were reproduced on this issue. The low value bore an example of the famous 1840 Penny Black by the line engraved process. The 1s. value bore the first embossed issue (1847) – the 1s. green, while the 1s.6d. stamp showed the first surface printed issue of 1855 – namely the 4d. carmine.

Issue date   18 September 1970.

Printer   Produced in sheets of 120 stamps by Harrison & Sons Ltd. Designer was David Gentleman.
Perforation 14 × 14.

Scarcity   Sales were approximately 72 million copies of the 5d., 16 million for the 9d. and 15 million for the 1s.6d. value.

Value   There are plenty of these sets available at about 40p.

Issue   ANNIVERSARIES – BRITISH LEGION

Description   Decimalisation of the currency took place early in 1971 and from now on all values are expressed in 'new' pence.

The British Legion was formed in 1921 to help ex-servicemen. The 3p stamp in this set shows three servicemen of 1921 and a nurse, together with a red poppy, emblem for the annual Poppy Day appeal held every November, which has raised many millions of pounds for welfare work and to support the British Legion village in Kent. The other two stamps marked the 1900th anniversary of York and the centenary of The Rugby Football Union.

Issue date   25 August 1971.

Printer   Harrison & Sons Ltd. Designer F. Wegner.
Printed on chalk surface paper.
Perforation 15 × 14.

Scarcity   Over 55 million copies were sold.

Value   This mint set now sells for about £1.

Issue   # BRITISH POLAR EXPLORERS

Description   Four stamps with portraits were issued in memory of some well-known British explorers dating back to the fourteenth century.

These comprised – 3p value Sir James Clark Ross, who discovered the sea named after him and established the North magnetic pole. His portrait came from a print owned by the Royal Geographical Society and is superimposed on a South Polar map printed in 1841. Sir Martin Frobisher appears on the 5p value, the illustration being taken from a painting in the Bodleian Library, Oxford. He sought a North West Passage when he entered the Arctic Circle in 1576.

Henry Hudson who discovered the bay named after him, appears on the $7\frac{1}{2}$p value, from a portrait by John Collyer. A photograph held by the Royal Geographical Society of Capt. Robert F. Scott, the South Pole hero, appears on the 9p value.

Issue date   16 February 1972.

Printer   Gravure printed by Harrison, with the Queen's head in gold and then embossed. Designer Marjorie Saynor. Perforation 14×15. Sheet size 100 stamps.

Scarcity   Over 5.5 million sets were sold.

Value   The mint set of four values sell for about £1.

Issue

BRITISH
ARCHITECTURE –
VILLAGE CHURCHES

Description Five stamps were issued in this set
showing various styles of village church
architecture over the centuries.
The 3p value illustrated St Andrew's,
Greensted-juxta-Ongar in Essex – one
of the earliest examples of Saxon
architecture and the only wooden
building to have survived from this
period. The 4p stamp showed a type of
Saxon tower built about 1,000 years
ago at All Saints, Earls Barton,
Northants. For the 5p value St
Andrew's, Letheringsett, Norwich
shows a round tower, evolved from the
use of flint set in mortar, due to lack of
stone. This is an almost exclusive
Norfolk and Suffolk style. A great
church from the Fens, St Andrew's,
Helpringham, Lincs, appears on the
$7\frac{1}{2}$p value and the final stamp (9p)
shows elaborate decoration on the
tower at St Mary the Virgin, Huish
Episcopi, Somerset.

Issue date 21 June 1972.

Printer   Printed photogravure Harrison & Sons Ltd in sheets of 100 stamps. Design by Ronald Maddox. Perforation 14 × 15.

Scarcity   53 million copies of the 3p stamp were sold.
The lowest quantity was about 5,463,000 of the 9p stamp.

Value   The mint set now sells for about £2.50.

Issue   # ROYAL SILVER WEDDING

Description   Two stamps were issued for this notable event, value 3p and 20p, and they were both similar in appearance. The aim of the designer was to achieve classical dignity and simplicity as often found on coins and medals, yet capture some of the spirit of the royal couple whose wedding was being commemorated. Norman Parkinson was commissioned to take the photographs which appear on the stamps and hand drawn lettering was used for the 'Silver Wedding' caption.

Issue date   20 November 1972.

Scarcity   Quantities sold: 59 million of the 3p value and 7 million for the 20p stamp.

Value   About 50p the mint pair. A souvenir pack was also produced comprising twelve pages of photographs and other royal family historical events, also the stamps. This is now valued at approximately £2.50.

Issue   # COUNTY CRICKET
1873–1973

Description   An issue of three low value stamps to mark the centenary of delegate meetings from first class cricketing counties which drew up rules regarding playing qualifications.
It was decided that a player would only be allowed to play for one county in any one season and that county could be either the location of his birth, his place of residence for two years or his family home.
The famous cricketer W. G. Grace was at his pre-eminence in the 1870s and

each of these stamps depicts the great master with sketches of him taken from *A Century of Grace*, a series of one hundred drawings by Harry Furniss.

Issue date   16 May 1973.

Printer   Photogravure process was used by Harrison & Sons Ltd. The designer was Edward Ripley.
Perforation 14 × 15. Printed in sheets of 100 stamps. A souvenir pack was sold at 60p.

Scarcity   Quantities sold were over 5 million of the 9p value, in excess of 6.5 million of the 7½p stamp and nearly 46 million of the 3p stamp.

Value   The mint set now realises about £1.50.

Issue   INIGO JONES – 400th ANNIVERSARY

Description   The 400th anniversary of the birth of the renowned architect Inigo Jones was recorded on four postage stamps depicting some of his work. Among his best-known buildings is St Paul's Church, Covent Garden, with its four massive Tuscan pillars. This is illustrated on one of the 3p values which was issued in se-tenant with another 3p stamp depicting court masque costumes, reminding us of Inigo's other great interest of designing for the stage. Two 5p se-tenant values shows another of his buildings, Prince's Lodging, Newmarket, which was demolished in the 1660s and a court masque stage scene.

The two theatrical themes are from work he undertook for a Ben Johnson masque.

Issue date   15 August 1973.

Printer   This issue was printed by lithography and typography by Bradbury Wilkinson, in sheets of 100. Perforation 15 × 14.

Scarcity   Over 21 million pairs of the 3p stamps were sold and about 5 million of the 5p pair.

Value   The four stamps sell for about £1.50.

Issue ROYAL WEDDING 1973

Description Two stamps value 3½p and 20p were issued for the wedding of the Queen's daughter Princess Anne to Capt. Mark Phillips. The illustration was taken from a photograph by Lord Lichfield, a cousin of the Queen.

Issue date 14 November 1973.

Printer Printed and rotary perforated by Harrison & Sons Ltd using the Jumelle press for the first time for a special issue. The Queen's head was printed in silver and then embossed.
Designed by Collis Clements and Edward Hughes.
Perforated 15 × 14. Sheets of 100 stamps.

Scarcity Sales were 54 million of the low value stamp and well over 7 million for the high value.

Value About 50p for the mint pair.

Issue	## CENTENARY BIRTH OF SIR WINSTON CHURCHILL
Description	A set of four stamps was issued to commemorate the birth of this famous statesman, depicting various phases of his long, varied and distinguished career. The 4½p stamp showed a portrait of him in the uniform of Lord Warden of the Cinque Ports to which he was appointed in 1941. A bowler hatted, cigar smoking Churchill as Prime Minister in 1940 appears on the 5½p. The 8p value goes further back into the past with a top hatted Churchill as Secretary for War and Air and the top value shows him as a war correspondent in South Africa 1899.
Issue date	9 October 1974.
Printer	Printed photogravure by Harrison & Sons Ltd. Designers Collis Clements and Edward Hughes. Perforation 14 × 15. Printed in sheets of 100 stamps.

Scarcity   54 million copies were sold of the low
value, about 9 million of the 5½p
stamp, around 8 million each of the 8p
and 10p stamps.
An illustrated biography of Churchill
was issued as a souvenir pack with the
stamps.

Value   The set of four mint stamps now sells
for around £1 and the souvenir pack
for £2.

Issue   # CHARITY STAMP 1975.
4½p POSTAGE + 1½p

Description The first and to date the only stamp
with a charity surcharge, was issued by
the Post Office as an experiment in aid
of organisations specialising in the
spheres of health and the handicapped.
The Trustees of the Charity Stamp
Fund were selected by the National
Council of Social Service and
appropriate benevolent organisations
appointed to administer and distribute
the proceeds of the 1½p premium
imposed on each stamp. Sadly the issue
was a relative failure with low sales and

the net sum realised for distribution was only £57,000. This was a disappointment for there were many examples of successful charity issues in various countries throughout the world.

Issue date   22 January 1975.

Printer   Printed by Harrison & Sons Ltd. Designed by Philip Sharland. Perforation 15 × 14. Sheets of 100 stamps.

Scarcity   It is believed that 30 million stamps were printed, but after four weeks the total sales at Post Offices were only 5.5 million. There were some later sales at philatelic counters.
The final total – about 7 million copies.

Value   There is little demand for this stamp, which now realises only about 15p.

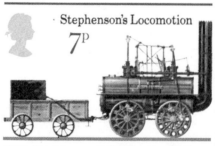

Issue   ## 150th ANNIVERSARY OF PUBLIC RAILWAYS

Description   This set of four stamps was issued to celebrate the passing of a century and a half since the inauguration of the first public steam railway. This was the Stockton to Darlington line and Stephenson's train *Locomotion* ran the first service on 27 August 1825. It carried twelve loaded coal wagons and twenty-two wagons equipped with seats. The engine and tender are illustrated on the 7p value.

Other notable trains shown on the stamps comprise:- The *Abbotsford* 1876, which was one of the first four locomotives for the new railway route between Settle and Carlisle.

This was on the 8p stamp. The 10p value bore a reproduction of the *Caerphilly Castle* 1923, which was the first of a new class of express trains on the Great Western Railway between London, Bristol, South Wales and the West Midlands. The engine is now preserved in the Science Museum, Kensington, London. The 12p stamp celebrates High Speed trains 1975 – prototypes for travel at over 100 m.p.h. on Inter-city routes.

Issue date	13 August 1975.
Printer	This set was printed by Waterlow & Sons Ltd. Designed by Brian Craker. Perforation 15×14. Sheets of 100 stamps.
Scarcity	Over 47 million stamps of the lowest value were sold. The other values achieved sales of between about 8 and 10 million each.
Value	The mint set sells for around 80p. PHQ cards for this set are quite rare and catalogued at around £30.

Issue	# CENTENARY OF THE ROYAL NATIONAL ROSE SOCIETY

Description Claimed to be the world's largest single flower Society, the Royal National Rose Society was established in 1876 and has its headquarters and twelve acres of gardens at St Albans, Hertfordshire.

To celebrate the centenary of the Society the Post Office commissioned four new stamps, all depicting popular roses. Named after the Queen Mother the variety 'Elizabeth of Glamis' a salmon pink floribunda appeared on the 8½p value stamp. 'Grandpa Dickson', a lemon yellow hybrid tea, adorned the 10p commemorative. On the 11p value was a shrub, 'Rosa Mundi', which has semi-double light crimson flowers. 'Sweet Briar' on the 13p value has single pink flowers with aromatic leaves.

Issue date 30 June 1976.

Printer Photogravure by Harrison & Sons Ltd. Designer Mrs Kristin Rosenberg.

Perforation 14 × 15. Printed in sheets
of 100 stamps.

Scarcity   Nearly 40 million copies of the low
value were sold. Between about 7 and
10 million of the other values were
purchased.

Value   The mint set now sells for
approximately £1.

Issue   BRITISH CULTURAL
TRADITIONS

Description   Two stamps were issued to celebrate the
800th anniversary of the Royal
National Eisteddfod, which is still held
annually in North and South Wales
alternately. The Welsh word is derived
from eistedd and means an assembly or
session and the original events were a
meeting of bards. Today the annual
meetings embrace music, poetry and
literature and one aim is to try and
preserve Welsh culture.

Members of the Druids order are bards who have won a National Eisteddfod chair or crown and from their members an Archdruid is elected.

The 8½p stamp illustrates an Archdruid in flowing robes. A harp is a traditional musical instrument of Wales and a harpist in appropriate costume appears on the 13p stamp.

As this set was intended to cover British traditions it also includes Morris dancing which is still practised in East Anglia and some other parts of England, on the 10p value and a Scots piper on the 11p stamp.

Issue date	4 August 1976.
Printer	Photogravure by Harrison & Sons Ltd. Designed by Marjorie Saynor. Perforation 14 × 15. Sheets of 100 stamps.
Scarcity	Over 38 million were sold of the low value and around 7 million of each of the others.
Value	About 70p for the mint set of four.

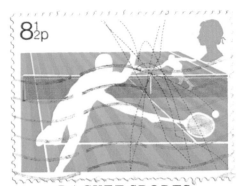

Issue   RACKET SPORTS

Description   The world famous Wimbledon Lawn
Tennis Championships celebrated their
centenary in 1977 and a set of four
stamps was issued illustrating lawn
tennis (8½p value), table tennis (10p
stamp), squash (11p) and badminton
(13p stamp).

The modern form of tennis is believed
to have originated in England and a
'Real Tennis' court was built at
Hampton Court by King Henry VIII in
1530. In the Victorian era, table tennis
became popular in universities and in
the services among officers. Birmingham
was the location of the World Table
Tennis Championships in 1977. Squash
developed from 'Fives' in the last
century and has become a very popular
keep fit sport in recent years. The
Badminton Association was formed in
1893.The game's name originates from
the seat of the Duke of Beaufort in
Gloucestershire.

Issue date   12 January 1977.

Printer	Harrison & Sons Ltd. Designed by Andrew Restall. Perforation 15 × 14. Sheets of 100.
Scarcity	About 37 million stamps were sold of the low value and approximately 7 million each of the other three stamps.
Value	This set sells for around 60p.

Issue	SILVER JUBILEE OF QUEEN ELIZABETH II REIGN
Description	Four multi-coloured stamps were issued to mark this important anniversary. The design is somewhat reminiscent of King George V's Jubilee set, but the format is slightly larger. The colour silver is included on each stamp and decorative initials ER appear prominently throughout.
Issue date	Four values appeared on 11 May 1977 and a fifth value (9p) was added on 15 June to cater for an increase in postal rates.

| **Printer** | Photogravure by Harrison & Sons Ltd. Designer Richard Guyatt. Perforation 15×14. Sheet size – 100 stamps. |

Scarcity   The late-issued 9p stamp sold over 42 million copies. Purchases of the other values were $8\frac{1}{2}$p, nearly 74 million; 10p, over 21 million; 11p, more than 19 million; top value 13p, 17.7 million.

Value   The five stamps in mint condition generally realise just under £1.

Issue   ENERGY RESOURCES

Description In 1978 North Sea oil and natural gas were beginning to be available in considerable quantities, so the Post Office chose to devote one of their special issues of stamps to Britain's energy resources of coal, gas, oil and electricity.

                 The theme of the 9p value was oil and it featured an artist's impression of a

North Sea production platform. The
10½p stamp showed a modern coal
pithead. Flame rising from the sea was
the theme of the 11p value and an
artistic version of a nuclear power
station and a uranium atom promoted
electricity on the 13p stamp.

Issue date 25 January 1978.

Printer Harrison & Sons Ltd by photogravure
process.
Designer Peter Murdoch. Perforation
14 × 15.
Printed in sheets of 100 stamps.

Scarcity Between 9 and 10 million copies were
sold of each of the three highest values.
The 9p stamp sold over 42 million
copies.

Value Approximately 60p the mint set.

Issue # BRITISH ARCHITECTURE – HISTORIC BUILDINGS

Description Royal Palaces and Castles were
featured on this set as follows:-
9p – Tower of London celebrating its

900th anniversary; illustrated is the
White Tower where the Crown Jewels
are displayed.

10½p – Holyroodhouse, Edinburgh,
built by James V.

11p – Caernarvon Castle, where the
Prince of Wales was invested.

13p – The Great Gatehouse, Hampton
Court, near London. Built 1520.

A miniature sheet of these four stamps
was also issued with a premium of 10p
which was devoted to the funds of the
London 1980 International Stamp
Exhibition.

Issue date   1 March 1978.

Printer   Harrison & Sons Ltd. Designer Ronald
Maddox. Miniature sheet designed by
Jeffery Matthews. Perforation 15 × 14.
Stamps in sheets of 100.

Scarcity   Nearly 44 million copies of the 9p value
were sold. The other three values sold
between about 10 and 11 million copies
each.

Value   The set of four stamps sells for around
60p and the miniature sheet for under
£1.

Issue	## 25th ANNIVERSARY OF THE CORONATION
Description	Four luxurious-looking stamps, printed in gold and other rich-looking colours were issued for this important milestone in the monarchy. The Coronation Regalia were the subjects chosen to be illustrated. Part of the State Coach appeared on the 9p value. This vehicle was built for George III and has been used for every Coronation since that of George IV. Worn only during the Coronation service, the St Edward's Crown is set with diamonds, rubies, emeralds, sapphires and pearls. This treasure is illustrated on the 10½p stamp. A gold globe circled with a band of precious stones, with a large amethyst beneath a jewelled cross, comprises the Orb, reproduced on the 11p value. The Imperial State Crown appears on the top value (13p). Originally made for Queen Victoria's Coronation, it is encrusted with diamonds and precious stones.
Issue date	31 May 1978.

Printer   Photogravure by Harrison & Sons Ltd.
Designer Jeffery Matthews.
Perforation 14 × 15. Printed in sheets
of 100.

Scarcity   Over 66 million copies of the 9p stamp
were purchased and around 15 million
each of the others.

Value   This mint set costs about 60p.

Issue   ## CYCLING
                 ## CENTENARIES

Description The Cyclist Touring Club and the
British Cycling Federation both
celebrated their centenaries in 1978 and
to mark these milestones a set of four
stamps was issued showing examples of
bicycles manufactured in the U.K. over
the years.
'Penny-farthings' were hazardous
bikes to ride, but in 1884 a low-built
safety bicycle with the rear wheel
operated by a chain drive, was
invented. Both of these forms of
transport are illustrated on the 9p
stamp. Touring by bike became
popular in the 1920s as can be seen on
the 10½p value. The most dramatic

change of style came about in 1962 with the introduction of Moulton's open frame and smaller 16-inch wheels (see 11p stamp). Road-racers are shown on the 13p stamp.

Issue date   2 August 1978.

Printer   Harrison & Sons Ltd. Designer Fritz Wegner.
Perforation 15 × 14. Printed sheets of 100.

Scarcity   Nearly 45 million copies of the low value were sold. The other stamps sold between 11 and nearly 13 million each.

Value   Mint sets of this issue sell for about 60p.

Issue   BRITISH DOGS

Description   This series is a continuation of an annual animal theme for stamps commenced in 1977.
The issue date coincided with the annual Cruft's Dog Show held in London under the auspices of the Kennel Club. This is considered to be the best-known dog event in the

world and at the time 10,000 dogs participated.

Four popular British breeds were chosen to appear on the stamps, namely Old English Sheep Dog (9p stamp), Welsh Springer Spaniel (10½p), West Highland Terrier (11p) and Irish Setter (13p).

Issue date   7 February 1979.

Printer   Photogravure by Harrison & Sons Ltd. Designed by Peter Barrett whose pet spaniel 'Charlie' was the subject for the 10½p stamp. Perforated 15 × 14. Printed in sheets of 100.

Scarcity   Nearly 50 million copies of the low value stamp were sold. The others achieved figures of between approximately 14 and 15 million.

Value   The set sells for about 65p.

Issue   # INTERNATIONAL YEAR OF THE CHILD

Description   The year 1979 was designated The Year of the Child by the United Nations General Assembly as it was the twentieth anniversary of the Declaration of the Rights of the Child. A set of four stamps was issued, each bearing a drawing of a favourite character from a famous children's book.

Jemima Puddleduck, Peter Rabbit and Squirrel Nutkin from Beatrix Potter's *The Tale of Peter Rabbit* appeared on the 9p stamp.

The drawing on the 10½p value was from *The Wind in the Willows* by Kenneth Grahame and showed Toad, Badger, Rat and Mole.

Eeyore, Christopher Robin and Piglet from *Winnie the Pooh* by A. A. Milne appeared on the 11p stamp and the quartet was completed by Alice, the Cheshire Cat and the Mad Hatter from Lewis Carroll's *Alice's Adventures in Wonderland* (13p stamp).

Issue date 11 July 1979.

Printer Photogravure by Harrison & Sons Ltd. Designed by Edward Hughes. Perforation 14 × 15. Sheets of 100 stamps.

Scarcity Sales of the low value totalled nearly 55 million copies. The other stamps all sold about 18 to 19 million each.

Value Approximately 70p for the mint set of four.

Issue	**CENTENARY OF DEATH OF SIR ROWLAND HILL**

Description   Sir Rowland Hill introduced Uniform Penny Postage in 1840, which reduced the prepaid cost of sending a letter weighing up to half an ounce anywhere in Britain to 1d. The new tariff was extremely popular and in 1840 alone more than double the mail was carried compared with the previous year.

A portrait of Hill appeared on the 10p stamp. A bellman in scarlet uniform of the General Post adorned the 11½p value. A postman of about 1839, in blue uniform, appeared on the 13p value and the 15p stamp depicted a Victorian lady and child, carrying letters.

Issue date   22 August 1979.

A miniature sheet with these four stamps was issued on 24 October, 1979. This carried a premium of 10p for the funds of the London 1980 Stamp Exhibition.

Printer   Photogravure by Harrison & Sons Ltd. Designed by Eric Stemp. Perforation 14 × 15. Printed in sheets of 100 stamps.

Scarcity   The 10p value sold over 74 million copies. About 18 million copies of each of the other values were purchased.

Value   Mint set 70p. Miniature sheet £1.

Issue   ## LONDON 1980 STAMP EXHIBITION

Description   A single stamp was chosen for this event. The format was considerably larger than normal and the face value (50p) higher than customary. The design depicted many famous London buildings including Nelson's Column, Westminster Abbey, Eros, Big Ben, St Paul's Cathedral, the Tower of London and Tower Bridge.
Some liberties were taken with scale and geographical location in order to achieve an effective view from the south bank of the River Thames.

Issue date   9 April 1980.
A miniature sheet was also issued on 7 May 1980 and this was sold at a premium of 25p for exhibition funds.

Printer   Printed by Harrison & Sons Ltd in
                sheets of 50. The miniature sheets were
                printed 18 up. Perforation 15 × 14.
                Designed by Jeffery Matthews,
                engraved by Geoffrey Holt.

Scarcity   Nearly 25 million copies of the stamp
                were sold and about 3.5 million
                miniature sheets.

Value   About 65p for the stamp and just under
                £1 for the miniature sheet.

Issue   ## BRITISH MUSICAL
                CONDUCTORS

Description Four eminent orchestral conductors
                were featured in this set which aimed to
                promote the musical heritage of Great
                Britain. A portrait of Sir Henry Wood
                who was the founder of the Promenade
                series of concerts held in London every
                year, appeared on the 12p stamp. After
                Sir Henry's death in 1944 his concerts
                were carried on for many years by Sir
                Malcolm Sargent, who appeared on the
                15p stamp and was also well-known for
                his work with choirs, particularly the

Royal Choral Society. The 13½p stamp was devoted to Sir Thomas Beecham who did much to help with the revival of opera in England. Shown on the top value (17½p) was Sir John Barbirolli who conducted the renowned Halle Orchestra.

Issue date   10 September 1980.

Printer   Photogravure by Harrison & Sons Ltd. Designed by Peter Gauld. Perforation 14×15. Printed in sheets of 100.

Scarcity   Over 45 million copies of the 12p stamp were sold. Figures for the other three values were around 10 million copies each.

Value   The mint set generally sells for just under £1.

Issue   BRITISH SPORTING CENTENARIES

Description   Athletics, Rugby Union, Boxing and
Cricket all celebrated notable
centenaries during 1980 and these were
the subject of four new stamps. The
Amateur Athletic Association was
founded in April 1880 (12p stamp). The
Welsh Rugby Union was established at
Neath towards the end of the 1880–1
season (13½p stamp).
The Amateur Boxing Association was
formed in the early part of 1880 and the
15p issue depicts two boxers in an
aggressive pose.
England played Australia in the first
Test match at the Oval, London,
during September 1880, so the top
value in the set (17½p) illustrated a
batsman.

Issue date   10 October 1980.

Printer   The House of Questa produced these
stamps by lithography. The designer
was Robert Goldsmith. Perforation
14 × 14.5
Printed in sheets of 100.

Scarcity   Well over 45 million copies of the low
value were sold. The other three stamps
sold between 10 and 11 million copies
each.

Value   The mint set sells for around 80p.

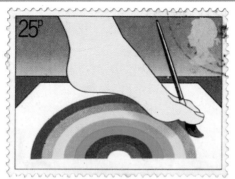

Issue

INTERNATIONAL YEAR OF DISABLED PEOPLE

Description   Chosen by the United Nations General Assembly 1981 was designated the International Year of Disabled People and the Post Office special issue of four stamps featured various methods of combating disabilities. For example the 14p stamp showed in diagramatic form, a guide dog with a blind man. People who were hard of hearing were reminded about the sign language with hands spelling 'deaf' on the 18p stamp. A disabled man in a wheelchair appeared on the 22p value and foot painting by a disabled artist was on the 25p stamp.

Issue date   25 March 1981.

Printer   Photogravure by Harrison & Sons Ltd. Designer John Gibbs. Perforated 15 × 14. Sheets of 100 stamps.

Scarcity   Over 43 million copies of the low value were sold. Totals for the other values were around 10 million each.

Value   An average price for this mint set is just over £1.

Issue   25th ANNIVERSARY OF
             DUKE OF EDINBURGH'S
             AWARD SCHEME

Description   Originally established on an
               experimental basis, over 1.5 million
               young people (ages between 14 and 25
               years) from the UK and overseas
               participated in the Duke of
               Edinburgh's Award Scheme in the first
               twenty-five years. The varied activities
               provided pleasure, satisfaction and a
               challenge to those who entered the
               scheme, thus ensuring its success.
               Themes of the four stamps were
               'Expeditions' (14p value), 'Skills'
               (18p), 'Service to the Public' (22p) and
               'Recreation' (25p stamp).

Issue date   12 August 1981.

Printer   John Waddington Ltd printed this set
             by lithography and it was the first
             special issue to be undertaken by the
             firm.
             The stamps were designed by Philip
             Sharland.
             Perforation 14 × 14. Printed in sheets
             of 100.

Scarcity   Quantities sold were approximately 43 million of the low value and around 10 million each of the other three values.

Value   Current price of this set is about £1.30.

Issue   YOUTH ORGANISATIONS

Description   A quartet of stamps commemorated important anniversaries in the life of prominent youth organisations. The 15½p value depicted the Boys' Brigade with a saluting youngster and a drummer. This organisation was founded in 1883 by William Alexander Smith. The Girls' Brigade illustrated by two stalwarts on the 19½p stamp, came about in 1965 following the amalgamation of three different organisations. Lord Baden-Powell, hero of Mafeking, held his first Scout Camp in 1907. The 26p stamp marked the 75th anniversary.

After the formation of the Scouts there was soon a demand for a similar organisation for girls. The Girl Guides Association was formed in 1910. The

29p stamp is devoted to the Girl Guide movement.

Issue date 24 March 1982.

Printer Photogravure by Harrison & Sons Ltd. Designed by Brian Saunders. Perforation 15 × 14. Printed in sheets of 100 stamps.

Scarcity About 40 million copies of the low value were sold and between 8 and 9 million each of the other three stamps.

Value About £1.70 for the mint set of four stamps.

LORD FISHER/HMS DREADNOUGHT

Issue BRITISH MARITIME HISTORY

Description The English Tourist Board designated 1982 as 'Maritime Heritage Year' in recognition of Britain's long naval and maritime traditions.
Many interesting events were organised culminating in the raising of the *Mary Rose*.
This 600-ton vessel capsized,

waiting for the French invasion fleet. An artist's impression of the ship and Henry VIII appeared on the 15½p stamp. Admiral Blake who fought with the Commonwealth Navy when the English Channel was threatened by the Dutch, appeared on the 19½p stamp with the ship *Triumph*. Lord Nelson and HMS *Victory* were on the 24p stamp. Heroes of the twentieth century were depicted on 26p and 29p stamps, namely Lord Fisher and HMS *Dreadnought* and Viscount Cunningham with his flagship HMS *Warspite*.

Issue date   16 June 1982.

Printer   Photogravure by Harrison & Sons Ltd. Designer Marjorie Saynor. Engraving by Czeslaw Slania. Perforation 15×14. Printed in sheets of 100.

Scarcity   Nearly 44 million copies were sold of the low value. The high value sold nearly 9 million copies and the others around 10–11 million.

Value   About £1.50 for the mint set of five stamps.

Issue	INFORMATION TECHNOLOGY
Description	An international conference held in 1982 created the opportunity for the Post Office to produce a pair of stamps for Information Technology Year. These were an unusual size being much longer than normal and not very deep. Both had three illustrations showing progress in communications. On the 15½p stamp were some Egyptian hieroglyphics, the British Library for research and a word processor. The 26p stamp had a Prestel viewdataset, a communications satellite and a laser light-pen.
Issue date	8 September 1982.
Printer	Harrison & Sons Ltd. Designers Brian Delaney and Darrell Ireland. Perforation 14 × 15. Sheets of 60.
Scarcity	33 million copies were sold of the low value and nearly 8 million of the 26p stamp.
Value	The mint pair sell for about 80p.

| Issue | **BRITISH RIVER FISH** |

Description   Another set of stamps with fauna and wildlife as a theme; devoted to what are considered to represent some of the most popular and important species of British river fish.

Fishing is a very popular pastime with a wide cross-section of the public and this issue co-incided with the tercentenary of the death of Izaak Walton, author of *The Compleat Angler* claimed to be one of the best books devoted to angling.

There were four stamps in the set depicting salmon (15½p stamp), pike (19½p), trout (26p) and perch (29p).

Issue date   26 January 1983.

Printer   Harrison & Sons Ltd. Designer Alex Jardine.
Perforated 15 × 14. Printed in sheets of 100.

Scarcity   Sales of this issue were around 7 million copies each of the three top values and about 38 million for the low value.

Value   About £1.30 per mint set.

Issue	**UNIFORMS OF THE BRITISH ARMY**

Description Five stamps were thought necessary to illustrate some of the British Army uniforms through the ages and to commemorate the 350th anniversary of the raising of the senior infantry regiment of the line – the Royal Scots Guards. A pikeman of this regiment was shown on the 16p stamp in a type of uniform which was intended to deflect musket balls.

A redcoat fusilier and ensign of the mid-eighteenth-century Royal Welsh Fusiliers were pictured on the 20½p stamp. Riflemen of the 95th Rifles (The Royal Green Jackets, 1805) appeared on the 26p stamp. The Irish Guards of 1900 with a sergeant in khaki service uniform and a guardsman in full dress uniform adorned the 28p value, while the top value (31p) illustrated contemporary paratroopers of the Parachute Regiment.

Issue date 6 July 1983.

Printer Harrison & Sons Ltd. Designed by Eric Stemp.

Perforation 14 × 15. Printed in sheets of 100.

Scarcity Sales of the low value were about 41 million. The next most popular was the 26p at over 10 million. The other values sold between about 7 and 8 million.

Value About £2 is the current price of this set.

Issue ## BRITISH GARDENS

Description Marking the bicentenary of the death of 'Capability' Brown the renowned landscape gardener, four stamps featured well-known British gardens. Pitmedden Garden, north of Aberdeen, on the 31p stamp, is an excellent example of a Tudor garden with clipped hedges and water features. Originally laid out by Sir Alexander Seton in 1675, this masterpiece includes three parterres taken from designs possibly used in the gardens at the Palace of Holyroodhouse, Edinburgh, in 1647. The other gardens of different centuries are eighteenth-century Blenheim an example of 'Capability' Brown's work (28p stamp); nineteenth-century Biddulph Grange, near Stoke-on-Trent, a 15-acre high Victorian garden conceived by James Bateman (20½p) and Sissinghurst, near Tunbridge Wells, Kent, created by Vita Sackville-West and her husband, Sir Harold Nicholson (16p stamp).

Issue date   24 August 1983.

Printer   Lithographed by John Waddington Ltd. Design by Liz Butler. Perforation 14 × 14. Printed in sheets of 100 stamps.

Scarcity   40 million copies were sold of the low value and about 7 million each of the others.

Value   This mint set sells for about £1.50.

Issue   BRITISH FAIRS

Description   Early fairs date back to Roman times and were mainly intended to create opportunities for rural inhabitants to sell or barter their produce and livestock. Later they also provided entertainment facilities from simple roundabouts and side shows to the sophisticated electronic rides of today. Some towns are still obliged to hold fairs on specific dates each year to comply with a Royal Charter granted to them centuries ago. The 31p value shows an early produce fair, while the 16p, 20½p and 28p stamps are devoted to entertainment.

Issue date   5 October 1983.

Printer   Harrison & Sons Ltd. Designer Andrew Restall.
Perforation 15 × 14. Sheets of 100.

Scarcity   Sales were about 38 million of the low value and between 7 and 8 million for the others.

Value   The mint set of four sells for around £1.80.

Issue   BRITISH CATTLE

Description   Two important events coincided with the issue of this set of five stamps; namely the bicentenary of the Royal Highland and Agricultural Society of Scotland, organisers of the first Royal Highland Show at Edinburgh in 1822

and the centenary of the Highland
Cattle Society. The 16p stamp shows a
Highland Cow which is able to
withstand very severe winters.
The Chillingham Wild Bull, shown on
the 20½p stamp, at Chillingham Park,
Northumberland, has remained
uncrossed with domestic cattle for 700
years. However selective breeding of
cattle in some other parts of the
country began many years ago.
Examples included the Hereford Bull
on the 26p value. Other breeds shown
on this set were the very hardy Welsh
Black Bull (28p stamp) and the Irish
Moiled Cow (31p).

Issue date   6 March 1984.

Printer   Photogravure by Harrison & Sons Ltd.
Designed by Barry Driscoll.
Perforation 15 × 14.
Printed in sheets of 100 stamps.

Scarcity   Quantity sold over 36 million of the 16p
stamp and around 7 million of the
others.

Value   The set of five mint stamps sells for
about £2.

Issue	**GREENWICH MERIDIAN CENTENARY**

Description In 1884 an international conference at Washington, attended by delegates from twenty-five countries, agreed to accept that the meridian longitude or 0° should pass through the Royal Observatory in south east London and set the standard for Greenwich Mean Time.

To commemorate the centenary of GMT four stamps were issued. These showed a view of the Observatory on the 28p value; the telescope designed by Sir George Airy and installed in the Observatory in 1850 appears on the 31p stamp. The other two values depicted a view of the earth from Apollo II on the 16p stamp and a Navigational Chart of the English Channel (20½p).

Issue date 26 June 1984.

Printer Lithography by the House of Questa. Designed by Howard Waller. Perforation 14 × 14.5. Printed in sheets of 100.

Scarcity Quantities sold were about 36 million of the low value and 6 to 7 million of the others.

Value Mint sets of four sell for around £2.

Issue   CHRISTMAS 1984

Description   A set of 5 stamps was issued to
                   celebrate the festive season in 1984. The
                   designer Yvonne Gilbert, was asked to
                   imagine herself as a photographer back
                   in the past, commissioned to record the
                   birth of Christ for posterity. The result
                   was very successful and some quite
                   realistic portraits were achieved. The
                   13p value showed the Holy Family; 17p
                   Arrival in Bethlehem; 22p Shepherd
                   and Lamb; 31p Virgin and Child and
                   the top value, 34p, Offering of
                   Frankincense.

Issue date   20 November 1984.

Printer   Printed by Harrison & Sons Ltd.
                   Perforated 15 × 14. Printed in sheets of
                   100.

Scarcity   Sales exceeded 250 million for the low
                   value, plus 120 million in the discount
                   rate booklets of 20 stamps, which were
                   offered at £2.30. The 17p value sold 148
                   million. The other three values between
                   about 12 and 16 million each.

Value   One of the better Christmas issues.
                   Sells for about £2.

Issue	**BRITISH FILM YEAR 1985**
Description	To commemorate British Film Year and the anniversary of the invention of the negative/positive photography process, the Department of Trade & Industry and the Film Institute sponsored a set of five stamps depicting famous film stars, all of whom were deceased at the time of issue, as tradition prevents depicting images of living persons on British stamps, except for members of the Royal family. Illustrated is the 31p value showing a photograph by Angus McBean of Vivien Leigh, renowned for her appearance as Scarlett O'Hara in *Gone with the Wind*. Peter Sellers appeared on the 17p value, David Niven on the 22p, Charlie Chaplin 29p and Alfred Hitchcock 34p.
Issue date	8 October 1985.
Printer	The stamps were printed in an unusual square size by Harrison & Sons Ltd and perforated 14.5 × 14.5. They were also

issued in a 24 page souvenir book with illustrations.

Scarcity   The Vivien Leigh stamp sold 7.1 million copies.

Value   The mint set of five sells for about £3.

Issue   60th BIRTHDAY OF QUEEN ELIZABETH II

Description   Portraits from six decades of the Queen's life arranged on a se-tenant pair of stamps made an attractive issue of two values, 17p and 34p. The illustrations show Her Majesty at the age of two from a photograh by Marcus Adams; as a sixteen-year-old, after becoming Colonel of the Grenadier Guards, from a portrait by Cecil Beaton; Dorothy Wilding provided the 1952 photograph which was also used on the first definitive issue of the Queen's reign. After the Queen's Birthday Parade (Trooping of the Colour) in 1958 a photograph was taken of Her Majesty on the balcony of Buckingham Palace. The penultimate

picture is by Photo Source and was
taken at Badminton Horse Trials in
1973. The final portrait (date 1982) is by
Snowdon.

Issue date   21 April 1986.

Printer   Photogravure by Harrison & Sons Ltd.
Designed by J. Matthews. Perforation
15×14. Printed in sheets of 100.

Scarcity   Quantity sold – 77 million of the 17p
stamp and 16.4 million of the 34p
value.

Value   About £1.50 for the mint set.

Issue   # EUROPA NATURE CONSERVATION

Description   Four stamps were issued illustrating
endangered species of animals. The 34p
value showed the Natterjack Toad,
which is found in sand dunes on the
coasts of North West England and East
Anglia. It moves by hopping and
running, not jumping, and has
disappeared from many former haunts
due to the destruction of habitat, but

has moved to new areas, which has resulted in road signs warning of migrating toads.
The other values show:- 17p Barn Owl; 22p Pine Marten; 31p Wild Cat.

Issue date   20 May 1986.

Printer   Photogravure by Harrison & Sons Ltd.
Designed by K. Lilly.
Perforation 14.5 × 14. Printed in sheets of 100.

Scarcity   Sales of the 17p stamp were about 36 million copies. The other values sold around 6 million copies each.

Value   About £1.50 the set.

Issue   # SPORTS ORGANISATIONS

Description   The centenaries of three sports organisations were marked by the issue of stamps designed to emphasise activity. Gymnastics appeared on the 18p value for the British Amateur Gymnastics Association. Downhill skiing on the 26p issue. A girl making a

stylish backhand stroke was featured
on the 31p stamp for the Lawn Tennis
Association's centenary and a
footballer was pictured on the 34p
stamp for the 100th anniversary of the
Football League.

Issue date   22 March 1988.

Printer   Harrison & Sons Ltd. Designer J.
Sutton.
Perforation 14.5×14.5. Printed in
sheets of 100.

Scarcity   Quantity printed not available.

Value   About £1.50 for the three mint stamps.

Issue   FAMOUS TRAINS

Description   To celebrate the 150th year since the
Great Western Railway Company was
established, a set of five stamps were
issued depicting well-known trains.
These comprised the Flying Scotsman
(17p stamp), The Golden Arrow (22p
value), The Cheltenham Flyer (29p),
The Royal Scot (31p) and the Cornish
Riviera (34p). The action-packed

illustrations appealed particularly to train collector enthusiasts and thematic specialists.

Issue date   22 January 1985.

Printer   Harrison & Sons Ltd. Designer T. Cuneo.
Perforation 15 × 14. Printed in sheets of 100 stamps.

Scarcity   Quantity printed not available.

Value   The mint set of five values sells for around £2.50.

Issue   ## ORDER OF THE THISTLE

Description   To celebrate the 300th anniversary of the revival of the Order of the Thistle, which occurred in 1687 by James II, stamps depicting various arms and a heraldic banner were issued. The 18p stamp bore the arms of the Lord Lyon King of Arms; the Scottish Heraldic Banner of Prince Charles appeared on the 22p stamp. The other two stamps had examples of the use of contemporary arms by corporations, namely the arms of the Royal Scottish Academy of Painting, Sculpture and Architecture on the 31p stamp and arms of the Royal Society of Edinburgh (34p stamp).

Issue date   21 July 1987.

Printer   Harrison & Sons Ltd. Designer Jeffery Matthews.
Perforation 14.5 × 14.5. Printed in sheets of 100.

Scarcity   Sale figures not available.

Value   About £1.80 will buy this set of four mint stamps.

Issue   ## 150th ANNIVERSARY OF ACCESSION OF QUEEN VICTORIA

Description   The accession to the throne of Queen Victoria 150 years previously was marked by the issue of four stamps showing important people and events during her reign. These range from the building of Crystal Palace and Grace

Darling on the 18p value to Mrs Beeton's *Book of Household Management*, the liner *Great Eastern* and Prince Albert on the 22p stamp (illustrated). The other two stamps were 31p, the Albert Memorial and Disraeli, and 34p – the Diamond Jubilee emblem and the Relief of Mafeking.

Issue date 8 September 1987.

Printer Harrison & Sons Ltd produced this set in combined photogravure and intaglio, using a Jumelle printing press. Designed by M.Dempsey. Perforation 15 × 14. Printed in sheets of 100.

Scarcity Figures not available for quantities sold.

Value The mint set of four values sells for about £1.60.

Issue EUROPA – TRANSPORT & MAIL SERVICES IN 1930s

Description The theme for the four stamps in this set is means of transport and communication. The design is in the style of travel posters of fifty years ago and the 18p value shows an artist's impression of 'Mallard', an engine which held the world steam train speed record in 1938. In the same year the largest liner ever built – the *Queen Elizabeth* was launched (26p). Luxury travel for over sixty passengers on a Glasgow tram is on the 31p stamp and the top value (34p) shows a Handley Page airliner of Imperial Airways which served routes to Europe and places in the British Empire at speeds of 110 mph.

Issue date   10 May 1988.

Printer   Photogravure by Harrison & Sons Ltd. Designed by M. Dempsey. Perforation 15×14. Printed in sheets of 100 stamps.

Scarcity   Sales figures are not available.

Value   The mint set of four sells for about £2.

Issue   # BICENTENARY OF AUSTRALIAN SETTLEMENT

Description   This was the first British joint issue with another postal administration, and stamps of almost identical design were issued by Australia Post on the same day.

There were two designs each for the 18p and 34p stamps. The lower value was printed se-tenant throughout the sheets, one stamp showing an early settler and a sailing clipper with a background of the Australian flag and the other depicted the Australian and British Parliament buildings and the Queen's head.

The 34p se-tenant pair showed an action picture of W. G. Grace, the famous cricketer, plus a tennis racquet and the Australian flag, while the second stamp was devoted to entertainment with illustrations of John Lennon, Sydney Opera House and a bust of Shakespeare.

Issue date   21 June 1988.

Printer   Lithography by the House of Questa. Designed by Garry Emery. Perforation 14.5×14.5. Printed in sheets of 100 stamps.

Scarcity   The quantity sold is not available.

Value   This set sells for about £1.50.

Issue	# CENTENARY OF DEATH OF EDWARD LEAR
Description	The artist and author Edward Lear was best known as a writer of nonsense verse, but was also a landscape painter and travel writer. The four stamps reproduce comic drawings from his books, with some verse, as follows: 19p stamp *The owl and the pussy-cat*; 27p stamp – *Edward Lear as a bird* (self-portrait); 32p stamp – *Cat*; 35p stamp – *There was a young lady whose bonnet* . . .
Issue date	6–27 September 1988.
Printer	Photogravure by Harrison & Sons Ltd. All the stamps were printed on a cream background in black and one second colour. Designed by Malcolm Swartridge and S. Dew. Perforation 15 × 14. Sheets of 100 stamps.
Scarcity	Quantity sold – figure not available.
Value	The mint set of four sells for around £1.60. A miniature sheet incorporating the four stamps was also produced and sold at £1.35, the premium of 22p being devoted to supporting 'Stamp World London 90' – the International Stamp Exhibition.

Issue   # HIGH VALUES 1988

Description   Four new high value non-commemorative stamps were issued in 1988 depicting various well known old British castles.

The illustrations were based on a series of photographs taken by Prince Andrew, Duke of York, a keen amateur photographer. The best-known building, Windsor Castle, was featured on the £5 stamp. The £1 value showed Carrickfergus Castle in Northern Ireland.

Caernarvon Castle on the £1.50 stamp was the location where the Prince's brother, Prince Charles, was invested as Prince of Wales in 1969. The ancient fortress of Edinburgh Castle appeared on the £2 stamp.

These castles were also depicted on the first high value stamps (2/6, 5/-, 10/- and £1) of Queen Elizabeth's reign issued between 1955 and 1968.

Issue date   18 October 1988.

Printer   Printed intaglio (recess) by Harrison & Sons Ltd in sheets of 100. Perforation 15 × 14.

Availability   These stamps are still current and can be purchased from post offices at face value.

Issue   GREETINGS STAMPS

Description   A booklet of ten stamps with a 'Greetings' theme was a new enterprise by the Post Office. There were five different designs of 19p stamps featuring roses, cupid, yachts, fruit and a teddy bear.

Issue date   31 January 1989.

Printer   Photogravure by Harrison & Sons Ltd. Designed by P. Sutton. Perforation 15 × 14.

Scarcity   Quantity sold – not available.

Value   About £3 for the complete booklet.

FOOD AND FARMING YEAR 1989

Issue	## FOOD & FARMING YEAR
Description	Four stamps depicting fruit and vegetables (19p), meat products (27p), dairy products (32p) and cereal products (35p) were issued, to remind us that food is one of the UK's largest industries, which supplies about three-quarters of the nation's needs. The issue also marked the 150th anniversary of the Royal Agricultural Society and the centenary of the Ministry of Agriculture.
Issue date	7 March 1989.
Printer	Harrison & Sons Ltd. Designed by Sedley Place Ltd. Perforation 14 × 14.5. Printed in sheets of 100.
Scarcity	Quantity sold – not available.
Value	The mint set of four sells for about £1.80.

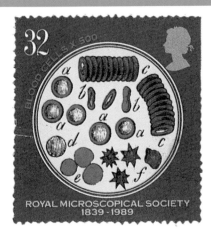

Issue	150th ANNIVERSARY OF ROYAL MICROSCOPICAL SOCIETY
Description	Stamps with a face value of 19p, 27p, 32p and 35p celebrate the 150th anniversary of the Royal Microscopical Society. These illustrate various organisms when seen under a microscope, namely a snow-flake magnified ten times, a Blue fly × 5; blood cells blown-up 500 times and a microchip enlarged 600 times.
Issue date	5 September 1989.
Printer	The House of Questa. Designed by Keith Bassford. Perforation 14 × 14.5.
Scarcity	Quantity sold – not available.
Value	The mint set of four sells for around £1.80.

Issue	**GALLANTRY AWARDS**

Description	Five stamps depicting prime gallantry awards were appropriately issued to coincide with the 50th anniversary of the introduction of the George Cross, the highest civilian decoration for bravery and the half century of two vital events of the Second World War, namely the Battle of Britain and the evacuation of Dunkirk. Each of the designs had a face value of 20p and they were issued in separate sheets and not se-tenant. The other medals illustrated were the Victoria Cross (the highest military award), the Distinguished Service Cross and Medal, the Military Cross and Medal and the Distinguished Flying Cross and Medal.
Issue date	11 September 1990.
Printer	Photogravure by Harrison & Sons Ltd. Designer John Gibbs with illustrations by John Harwood. Perforation 14.5. Printed in sheets of 100.
Availability	The stamps can be obtained at face value.

Issue	# GREETINGS STAMPS BOOKLET 1991
Description	Good luck symbols are incorporated in ten different stamp designs in a booklet. The stamps when viewed together form one overall picture and were designed to be appropriate for a variety of social mail and not limited to specific occasions. The booklets also contained twelve small labels with greetings messages ranging from 'Happy Birthday' to 'Congratulations'. The aim of these was to use them with the stamps to make them more specific. The stamps carried first class non-value indicators (NVI) and were available for inland use only. The overall size of the complete booklets was 69.5 mm × 95 mm and the stamps were folded twice along the perforations.
Issue date	5 February 1991.
Printer	Harrison & Sons Ltd by photogravure in a continuous reel on the Jumelle Press. Designed by Tony Meeuwissen. Perforation 15 × 14.
Availability	The books can be purchased price £2.20 from post offices and the British Philatelic Bureau.

Issue

SCIENTIFIC ACHIEVEMENTS

Description Four stamps honouring British scientific achievements. Two commemorated the bicentenaries of the births of Michael Faraday, renowned for his experiments with electricity, and Charles Babbage, whose calculating machine is regarded as the precursor of today's computers. Portraits of these men appeared on two variants of the 22p stamp.
The 31p value records work done by Sir Robert Watson-Watt on radar and the top value (37p) features the jet engine of Sir Frank Whittle which was first flown fifty years ago.

Issue date 5 March 1991.

Printer Photogravure by Harrison & Sons Ltd. Designers Peter Till (22p stamps) and John Harwood (31p and 37p). Perforation 14 × 15. Printed in sheets of 100.

Scarcity Quantity sold not known as the stamp was currently available at post offices during 1991.

Issue

'SMILES' GREETINGS STAMPS 1991

Description Following the popularity of the 1990 'Smiles' stamps, the Post Office reissued this series in 1991 with the same designs which comprised a teddy bear, Dennis the Menace, Punch, the Cheshire Cat, the Man in the Moon, the Laughing Policeman, the *Mona Lisa*, the Queen of Hearts, a clown, and Stan Laurel. The stamps were intended for long-term use and bore the first class post indicator in place of the 20p value on the previous issue. These stamps were issued in booklets of ten, together with twelve small perforated greetings messages.

Issue date 26 March 1991.

Printer Photogravure on the Jumelle press by Harrison & Sons Ltd. Designed by Michael Peters & Partners Ltd. Perforation 15 × 14.

Scarcity On long-term sale at face value from most post offices and some retailers.

CHANNEL ISLANDS

The offshore islands of Guernsey and Jersey, which lie close to the coast of France, have their own internal administration and established independent postal administrations, with their own distinctive stamps, on 1 October 1969.

For eleven years from 1958 both islands participated in the Great Britain regional issues produced by the U.K. Post Office with their own designs, including the head of Queen Elizabeth II, but without any indication of the country of origin. The two islands also issued 'emergency' stamps during the occupation of their territory by Germany between 1940 and 1945.

Guernsey and Jersey have both issued many attractive commemorative and definitive sets of stamps over the past two decades and examples are illustrated on the following pages.

Issue	# GUERNSEY 50th ANNIVERSARY OF OCCUPATION STAMPS
Description	Having over-run Northern France, a section of the German army invaded the Channel Islands at the end of June 1940 and for nearly five years occupied this British territory until liberation in May 1945. A shortage of current British postage stamps soon occurred and permission was given by the Germans for a local issue of stamps to be produced. The design depicted the arms of Guernsey and three values were issued ($\frac{1}{2}$d., 1d. and 2$\frac{1}{2}$d.). These stamps were reproduced on the fiftieth anniversary set.
Issue date	18 February 1991.
Printer	Offset lithography by BDT International. Designer Clive Abbott. Perforation 14. Printed in sheets of 20 stamps.
Availability	The three stamp values 37p, 53p and 57p were available at face value during 1991, from post offices in Guernsey.

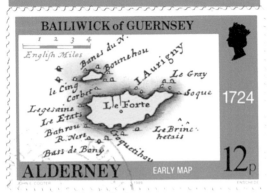

Issue   MAPS OF ALDERNEY

Description   Alderney, one of the smaller Channel
                   Islands, has its own States or
                   Parliament which legislates on internal
                   matters but is part of the Bailiwick of
                   Guernsey and since 1983, the Guernsey
                   Post Office has issued a series of
                   commemorative and some definitive
                   stamps which are valid in Alderney and
                   the rest of the Bailiwick.
                   The maps set includes a 12p value
                   depicting Moll's map of Alderney,
                   dated 1724, and commemorates the
                   250th anniversary of Bastide's survey
                   of Alderney.
                   The four other stamps in this set show
                   various antique maps and the latest
                   Ordnance Survey of the island.

Issue date   7 July 1989.

Printer   Litho by Euchede. Designer J. Cooter.
                   Perforation 14. Sheets of 50 stamps.

Value   About £2 for the set of five.

Issue	WILDLIFE PRESERVATION TRUST, JERSEY
Description	Founded in 1963 by Gerald Durrell, the well-known preservationist and author, the Jersey Wildlife Preservation Trust aims to build up breeding colonies of threatened species of small reptiles, mammals and birds. A set of four colourful stamps promoting the trust featured White Eared Pheasants (2p value), Thick-Billed parrots (2½p), Ursine Colobus Monkeys (7½p) and Ring-Tailed Lemurs (9p).
Issue date	12 March 1971.
Printer	Photogravure by Courvoisier of Switzerland. Designed by Jennifer Toombs. Perforation 11.5. Printed in sheets of 50.
Scarcity	Quantities printed were over one million copies of the two lowest values. About 230,000 of the 7½p stamp and approximately a quarter of a million copies of the 9p stamp.
Value	The mint set sells for around £10.

GLOSSARY OF
PHILATELIC TERMS

Adhesive postage stamp. Issued in 1840 the Penny Black and the 2d. Blue were the first stamps produced with a gum on the back which could be moistened and affixed to letters for the prepayment of postage.

Aerogrammes. Postal stationery printed on light-weight paper, suitable when folded for transmission by air at an economic cost. The original examples produced by Germany in 1923 required the affixation of adhesive stamps. Most examples now in use throughout the world have stamps pre-printed on them.

Airgraph. Introduced during the 1939–1945 war for the use of British forces serving overseas. Letters were written on special forms which were microfilmed at source and the films were then flown to London where prints were made and dispatched to addresses in special envelopes, by normal inland mail. Over a four-year period about 350 million airgraphs were handled.

Airmail. Letters and parcels dispatched by air.

Aniline. An ink that is fugitive and runs when immersed in water. Helps to prevent the cleaning and reuse of stamps.

Approvals. Stamps on cards or in booklets sent by dealers via the post, to clients for inspection, purchase or return.

Archer perforation. Henry Archer invented methods of separating stamps which had been printed in sheets. Initially his roulette method pierced the surface of the paper, but his later machine punched holes and removed the small discs of paper, which was more efficient.

Bilingual pairs. Two adjoining stamps with inscriptions in different languages.

Bisect. A stamp which has been cut in two equal parts and authorised for use at half the face value.

Bishop mark. A small circle divided into two parts, with the date in one half and the month in the other. Claimed to be the earliest dated postmark and named after the Postmaster General, Sir Henry Bishop, 1660–1663.

Bleed. Printing which runs off the edge of the paper.

Block. A group of unsevered stamps.

Bogus. A fictitious issue of stamps by a non-existent country or postal administration.

Booklet. A small group of stamps in a card or paper cover. Often sold from vending machines or non post office outlets.

Cachet. A printed or rubber-stamped message or design on the front of an envelope for some special event or circumstance.

Cancelled to order (CTO). Stamps which have not been through the normal postal service, but are cancelled carefully by the Post Office as a favour to collectors.

Cancellation. Defacement of a stamp by a postmark to indicate it has been used for postage and prevent reuse.

Censor marks. Mail censored in wartime is often resealed by the censor with a special label and a rubber stamp is applied to the envelope indicating that action has been taken.

Certified mail. A low-cost alternative to registered mail. A receipt is given by the post office and the recipient signs for the item on delivery. There is no check *en route*.

Charge marks. Handwritten indications or labels applied to mail where the postage has been underpaid or not paid in advance, or where some regulation has been infringed, and a sum of money is due on delivery.

Charity stamps. Postage stamps bearing a surcharge for a charitable project.

Check letters. The early issues of Great Britain stamps had letters in the lower corners, which were reversed in the upper corners to prevent matching up uncancelled sections of two previously used stamps.

Cinderella stamps. Any item resembling a stamp that does not fulfil a postal purpose, e.g. a receipt stamp.

Circular date stamp (CDS). A round postmark with single or double circle. Generally indicates place and date of posting.

Classic. Normally denotes stamps of interest issued during the nineteenth century.

Coil. Stamps dispensed from a roll in a vending machine.

Colour proof and trials. Stamp designs printed in different experimental colours, prior to a final selection.

Comb perforation. Here the perforating pins are arranged in a comb pattern with short vertical lines and long horizontal ones. Thus the sides and top row of the stamps are perforated in one operation.

Commemoratives. Stamps issued for a special event and generally only on sale for a limited period.

Composite stamps. Examples of these are where the design is spread over two or more stamps.

Counterfoil. Part of a stamp or a label retained by the dispatcher as a receipt.

Cover. An envelope or wrapper bearing stamps.

Crash cover. Mail salvaged from an aircraft or mail train which has been involved in an accident and crashed.

Cut to shape. A stamp printed on stationery or an embossed stamp which has been trimmed to the shape of the design.

Cylinder number. Minute numbers, often in the margins

of a sheet of stamps, which have been engraved on the cylinder used in photogravure printing.

Dead letter. Mail that cannot be delivered by the Post Office because the address is incomplete or the addressee cannot be traced.

Definitives. Ordinary postage stamps which are on general sale for an unlimited period.

Demonetised. Stamps no longer having postal validity and withdrawn from circulation.

Die. An original engraved piece of metal from which reproductions are made for the printing process.

Disinfected mail. In the eighteenth and nineteenth centuries it was thought that letters might carry disease and mail emanating from sources where there was plague were often disinfected on arrival from overseas.

Dockwra mark. William Dockwra devised a triangular mark in the seventeenth century to denote that postage had been prepaid.

Double letter. Letters comprising two sheets of paper, or one sheet and an envelope, were charged double postage prior to 1840. The term is also used to denote partial double impressions of check letters in the corners of early Great Britain stamps.

Duplex cancel. A handstamp where the postmark includes the date and an obliterating device.

Entire. A complete envelope with stamp(s), postmark and possibly a letter enclosed.

Error. A mistake in the design of a stamp.

Essay. Design for a new stamp which has not been adopted.

Facsimile. A copy of an original stamp, but not a forgery as it is marked to indicate its status.

Fine used (FU). Stamps cancelled with a light and neat postmark and being clean and complete in every respect.

First day cover. An envelope with new stamps postmarked on the first day of issue.

Fiscal stamps. Stamps used to collect taxes or duty payable to the state, as distinct from paying for postal service.

Flaw. A mistake made during the manufacture of a stamp.

Frama labels. Labels issued from a coin-operated machine manufactured by Frama of Switzerland, for the prepayment of postage.

Frank. A postmark or a mark indicating that an item is dispatched without charge.

Fugitive inks. These run or change colour when moistened.

Graphite lines. During early experiments in England with automatic sorting of mail, vertical black lines were printed on the back of certain stamps, to segregate first and second class mail.

Guide lines. Marks on a printing plate to guide an engraver when transferring impressions.

Gum. The adhesive product applied to the back of stamps.

Gutter. The space between stamps for the perforations or between rows of stamps in a sheet.

Gravure. An abbreviation for photogravure which is a process of printing from a photograph etched on a plate.

Handstamp. A postmark applied to a stamp by hand.

Hinge. A piece of gummed transparent paper used to affix a stamp to an album page. Generally supplied ready folded.

Imperforate. A stamp not perforated when printed and requiring to be cut from a sheet with scissors.

Imprimatur. In philately means the initial sheet produced from a finished printing plate.

International reply coupon (IRC). A method of sending reply postage with a letter going abroad. The coupons sold by many post offices throughout the world, can be exchanged in another country for stamps equivalent to the cost of surface postage.

Ivory head. Early British stamps where chemicals have produced an ivory cameo of Queen Victoria's head on the reverse side.

Key plate. The main plate of a stamp where two printings are required. The second plate often adds the value figure.

Killer. A heavy postmark which virtually obliterates some or all of the stamp design.

Kiloware. Used stamps on parts of envelopes or cards which are sold by commercial organisations or post offices by weight (kilograms) to collectors or dealers.

Laid paper. Paper used for printing stamps with a watermark of lines close together, either vertically or horizontally.

Late fee. An additional sum paid to the post office for the dispatch of mail after the normal closing time for night train dispatches.

Local stamps. Stamps valid only for a prescribed local service, sometimes issued by private carriers.

Maltese Cross. An eight-pointed cross once used by the Knights of Malta as their emblem. Adapted as the main obliterating device for cancelling the early British stamps.

Manuscript postmark. In the early days of adhesive postage stamps, some small post offices did not have date stamps, so officials wrote the place and date across stamps to cancel them. This also occasionally happens now in an emergency.

Margins. The paper around the edge of a sheet of stamps, or space between the design and the perforations on a stamp.

Maritime mail. Mail from naval vessels at sea, which is brought ashore for dispatch to destinations indicated.

Matched pair. Some Great Britain 1840 Penny Blacks and 1841 Penny Reds were printed from the same plates. Dedicated collectors like to acquire specimens of the two issues, from the same plate, having similar check letters.

Maximum cards. Picture postcards sometimes issued by a post office which are franked and postmarked with stamps relevant to the subject of the card.

Meter mark. A postmark and stamp specially printed all in one by a machine on a letter or label in an office, which has prepaid a lump sum for postage to the post office.

Miniature sheets. Small sheets comprising one or more perforated stamps with a wide surrounding margin. Often commemorating a special event and having an appropriate inscription.

Mint and **Mounted mint (MM)**. An unused stamp with complete gum, that is in perfect condition and worth a premium over mounted mint which is a stamp that has been attached to a hinge.

Mobile post office. A vehicle which has been equipped as a post office for special events etc.

Newspaper tax stamps. In the eighteenth and nineteenth centuries newspapers were taxed and the duty was paid by affixing a special stamp on the front page. When this tax had been paid the papers could be sent through the post without further charge. Thus people collect these items which are an example of 'Cinderella' collecting.

Numeral cancellations. The Maltese Cross was superseded by obliterators incorporating numbers which indicated the location of the posting office.

Obsolete. Stamps which are no longer current at the post office, but still valid to prepay postage.

Official mail. Government departments are sometimes exempt from paying postage on official correspondence. Formerly, the Inspector of Taxes always sent a post-free envelope to taxpayers when requiring a reply. This concession has been discontinued and now only the Collector of Taxes pays for reply postage!

Off-centre. A stamp with unequal margins, caused by faulty perforation or bad printing.

Offset litho. A modern version of lithography, where printing is not direct from a plate, but the ink is transferred to another roller from which the paper takes up the ink and is thus printed.

Omnibus issue. A series of stamps issued by a number of countries to record a particular event.

Overprint. Wording or an object printed on to a stamp after the initial printing.

Original gum. The adhesive applied originally when the stamp was first issued and not regummed at a later date.

Packet Mail. Mail delivered ashore from a government-run ship or a ship under contract to carry mail for the post office.

Paid postmark. When postage is prepaid in cash at a post office a postmark indicating that postage has been paid is often applied to mail in red ink. Particularly applies to bulk postings.

Pair. Two adjoining stamps (vertically or horizontally) which are unsevered.

Pane. Two or more stamps issued in booklets or part of a sheet of stamps.

Paquebot. A French word which translates as 'packet boat'. The Universal Postal Union adopted this word to indicate mail posted on board ship and taken ashore for onward transmission.

Perfin. Stamps perforated with a firm's initials as a security measure.

Penny post. Pioneered by William Dockwra in 1680 for the delivery of letters within a defined limited area. By the 1830s local penny post was available in many parts of the British Isles. Uniform penny post providing carriage by mail irrespective of distance in the UK of letters of up to half an ounce was introduced in January 1840.

Perforation. Holes punched in the margins between stamps to assist separation. Perforations are measured by the number of holes in a length of two centimetres.

Phosphor. To operate a scanner which sorted mail into first and second class categories and for automatic facing and cancelling, a phosphorous substance was applied to the surface of certain British stamps in the late 1950s. Subsequently phosphor bands were applied and then phosphorised paper used.

PHQ Cards. Since 1973 the British Post Office has issued a series of postcards reproducing newly issued stamps. The initials PHQ stand for Postal Headquarters.

Pictorial postmarks. Special events are sometimes recorded by the use of postmarks with appropriate illustrations.

Plate flaw. A damaged printing plate may reproduce a blemish on a stamp.

Plate number. A marginal notation on a sheet of stamps indicating the plate from which the stamps were printed.

Poached egg. Testing labels used on stamp vending machines by the British Post Office. So called because of the design.

Postage due. Post Office labels indicating the amount to be paid by the recipient of a letter or package, where postage has been underpaid or not paid.

Postal history. The study of information about the origins of postal services and their development.

Postal stationery. Envelopes, cards, wrappers and airletters issued by the Post Office bearing an indication that postage has been prepaid, or having imprinted stamps.

Post code. For the use of automatic sorting equipment, addresses in the UK are allocated a group of letters and numbers. Other countries sometimes use numbers only.

Postmark. A cancellation applied to stamps by hand or machine to indicate the district of posting, date and sometimes the time the item was handled.

Pre-adhesive. A term to describe an item of mail dispatched by post prior to the introduction of adhesive stamps.

Pre-cancel. Bulk posted mail sometimes bears a machine printed cancellation or handstamp indicating postage has been paid.

Presentation pack. A set of stamps with some description packed in a souvenir presentation.

Printed matter. Commercial papers, printed circulars and magazines qualifying for reduced rates of postage.

Printer's waste. Badly printed or spoilt specimens which should be destroyed by the printer.

Privilege envelope. Certain charitable organisations were granted reduced postal rate privileges in the nineteenth century. The term was also used during the Second World War for servicemen's mail which was not subject to censorship. The sender had to sign a statement on the outside of the envelope that the contents were entirely personal.

Provisionals. Stamps generally used for a short period only to solve an emergency or to fulfil a temporary shortage.

Quadrille paper. Paper watermarked with a series of crossed lines creating small squares.

Quartz lamp. An electric lamp which emits ultra-violet rays which cause fluorescence on contacting certain substances. The lamp is used for checking stamps for repairs etc.

Recess printing. Ink is forced into recesses or space engraved below the surface of a printing plate.

Recorded delivery. See **Certified mail**.

Re-entry. Damaged or worn parts of line-engraved plates are sometimes corrected or re-engraved to save making a new plate. If the work is inadequate, parts of the old matter are still visible, causing a duplication of an image.

Regionals. Stamps issued for parts of a country.

Regummed. Old and new stamps sometimes have new gum applied to the backs, to mislead collectors as to their value.

Remainders. After an issue of stamps has been taken off

sale, the remaining stock should be destroyed, but sometimes they are sold to philatelists at a cheap rate.

Reply postcards. Postal stationery comprising two adjoining cards, one of which is used by the sender and the other returned by the answering recipient.

Reprints. Stamps printed from the original plates once the stamps are no longer current.

Retouch. A minor correction undertaken by hand-engraving on a cylinder or plate.

Rotogravure. Another name for photogravure.

Rouletting. A method of separating stamps in a sheet by cutting or piercing the surface, rather than punching holes and removing small discs of paper.

Selvedge. The marginal paper around a sheet of stamps.

Se-tenant. In French this means 'joined together' and the expression is used by philatelists to describe adjoining stamps of differing values, design, colour, inscription or other material variation.

Set-off. Printing on the back of a sheet of stamps caused by contact with another sheet where the ink was wet.

Sheetlet. A small sheet with just a few stamps.

Silk thread paper. A type of safety paper with coloured threads of silk embedded.

Specimen stamps. Samples of new stamps.

Spoon cancels. Duplex cancellations used as an experiment in England and Wales between 1853 and 1860. So called because the date portion is oval in shape.

Squared circles. The first type of combined date and obliterating stamp used from 1879 had rectangular corners and concentric arcs surrounding a round date circle.

Strip. A row of three or more stamps.

Surcharge. An overprint on a stamp which alters the face value.

Tab. An addition to a stamp in the form of a coupon.

Tête-bêche. Another French idiom, which in the world of philately indicates a pair of stamps, one of which is upside-down.

Thematic collecting. A collection of stamps by specific subjects or themes.

Tin Can Mail. On the island of Niuafo'ou, Tonga there were difficulties in conveying mail from ships anchored off-shore owing to the surf. So islanders used cannisters to float letters to and fro and applied colourful cachets to them.

To pay labels. See **Postage due**.

Too late. A postmark or hand inscription explaining delay in delivery of mail which has missed the last dispatch of the day.

Traffic lights. Check dots in the margin of a sheet of stamps to ensure the colours have been printed correctly.

Transit postmarks. Postmarks applied during transmission between the dispatching and delivering offices.

Travelling Post Offices (TPO). Special long-distance railway trains had facilities for sorting mail *en route*. Late fee boxes were provided on some trains and special postmarks were used to indicate the use of the service.

Treaty Ports. From 1843 onwards some European powers had trading facilities in certain Chinese seaports and operated postal services.

Underprint. Stamps which have printed matter on the back. Also a feint pattern under the main design of a stamp for security reasons.

Ungummed. Certain countries with very hot, humid climates have issued stamps without gum. Another cause of lack of gum may be that the stamps have been stuck together and soaked to separate them.

Universal Postal Union (UPU). Founded in 1874, with headquarters in Berne, Switzerland, to facilitate postal co-operation among countries throughout the world.

Used. A stamp which has had postal use and cancelled with a postmark or in manuscript.

VFU = very fine used, i.e. cancelled with a light, clear and sharp postmark.

V-Mail. USA equivalent of the British airgraph service.

Value tablet. The space or panel on a stamp where the value figure is inscribed.

Vignette. A picture that gradually fades into the surrounding background.

Watermark. A pattern or device in paper which can be seen when exposed to light. Used generally as a security device.

Wing margin. A wide margin on one side of a stamp.

Wreck cover. An item of mail salvaged from a wrecked ship.

Zip code. The USA postcode.

INDEX